Praise for *Portrait of an Expatriate: A Lebanese-American Story*

"Capturing the full weight of this memoir feels almost impossible. It is lived tension, a quiet resilience, and a testament to what it means to belong to more than one world at once. Rooted in his personal journey of emigrating from Lebanon to the United States, Deek's story transcends the familiar arc of immigration. It invites us into the enduring duality of identity: the ache for a past that cannot be reclaimed and the determination to build a future that never fully lets go of its origins.

What emerges is not only a portrait of displacement but of formation. This is a story about becoming: becoming a leader not through title or ambition, but through a sustained commitment to values that do not waver. Persistence, patience, and quiet strength are woven together with a deep sense of purpose. At its core lies a profound love for people in community and a deep belief in processes, guided by integrity.

Even in moments of personal achievement, Deek's voice turns outward. His success is never solitary but rather communal. Mentors, colleagues, and family are not supporting characters but co-authors of his journey. In this way, the narrative becomes an offering, a tribute to those who shaped him and a guide for those who will follow.

For a new generation of leaders, this memoir is both an inspiration and an invitation. It reminds us that excellence in science and technology is never purely technical: Deek's values are grounded in a humanistic vision that transforms knowledge into service and ambition into meaningful leadership. Ultimately, this is more than a life story. It is a reflection on how to live with purpose, gratitude, and enduring impact."

—Katia Passerini, President of Gonzaga University

"This deeply felt memoir is an ode to the importance of familial and cultural values on his journey from battle scarred Lebanon to the city of Newark, New Jersey. Central to the narrative is Deek's academic trajectory at NJIT, rising to become Dean, then Provost and Senior Executive Vice President. It is a fascinating tale of how his leadership, intellectual drive, and ability to develop communities enabled the institution's rise to prominence. Deek's reflections on leadership are most insightful. His story will resonate with all expatriates, especially those of the Lebanese diaspora, who came to America and made an enduring impact."

—John Poate, Emeritus Senior Vice President
of Research, Colorado School of Mines

"A story of a young person coming to the United States and reaching success is not rare. What is unique about Deek's memoir is that he adopted, with love, his new country and learned its culture—maintaining his Lebanese identity. His definition of success exceeded personal gains. He cared about the success of others and mentored them to realize their own potential. He dedicated his life to serving others.

As someone who had the privilege to work closely with the author during the years of his service as Provost and Senior Executive Vice President, I can attest to the memoir's accuracy of details. With his consistent calm and determined demeanor, Deek motivated everyone to do their best and more. Along with his uncompromised dedication to high academic standards, rigor, equity, and integrity, his genuine care about students inspired innovations in both teaching and student support services. His support to faculty, especially the newly hired, led to high levels of productivity. Starting his day well before day break, the author's first encounters of the day were the grounds and custodial staff. He knew them by their names, listened to their personal stories, and interacted with them as friends and equals. Even though this meant longer days for him, his door was open to everyone.

His ability to conceptualize ideas and bring them to fruition was beyond remarkable. He was the maestro *par excellence* who conducted a flawless symphony during his years of service. My hope is that this memoir will reveal an alternative route based on hard work, empathy, inspiration, social connectivity, and basic family principles that lead to authentic fulfillment and enduring success."

—*Basil Baltzis, Professor of Chemical Engineering and former Senior Vice Provost for Academic Affairs & Student Services, NJIT*

"Deek's memoir tells the story of a young man from Lebanon who sets out to make a new life in America. After chronicling his early years in a war-torn country, he takes the reader along on his dizzying ride from an undergraduate student to the highest rung of the academic ladder. Deek deftly manages to navigate the dichotomy between assimilation and staying true to his Levantine cultural heritage. His is a tale of hope, of aspiration, and of the will to make it happen. The description of his journey is laced with introspective insights. His is a life well led. Throughout, his leitmotif could have been Goethe's adage: *Arbeite nur, die Freude kommt von selbst* (Keep working, the joy will come on its own)."

—*Urs Gauchat, Emeritus Dean of the College of Architecture and Design, NJIT*

Purple Breeze Press, LLC

Purple Breeze
PRESS

purplebreezepress.com
Portrait of an Expatriate: A Lebanese-American Story
© 2026 Fadi P. Deek

Library of Congress Cataloguing in Publication Data
Names: Deek, Fadi P., author
Title: *Portrait of an Expatriate: A Lebanese-American Story*
Description: First edition. | Purple Breeze Press, 2026

Library of Congress Control Number: 2026908171
ISBN Paperback: 979-8-9954928-0-1

Book designed by Streetlight Graphics

About Cover Page Photo: Fadi Pierre Deek and Maura Ann McShane venturing out of the ancient Phoenician harbor in Byblos on a small fishing boat on their engagement day, December 24, 1986.

Royalties from this book will be added to the Fadi Pierre and Maura Ann Deek Scholarship at New Jersey Institute of Technology.

Portrait of an Expatriate:

A Lebanese-American Story

Fadi P. Deek

Purple Breeze

PRESS

To my grandchildren, Charles and Isabelle

Lead the way and help guide those who come after you.

TABLE OF CONTENTS

INTRODUCTION: A Destination and a Journey 1

PART ONE: The Destination 5
    Chapter 1: Leaving My Homeland 7
    Chapter 2: West Toward a New Home 41
    Chapter 3: A Lebanese Student Abroad 55

PART TWO: The Journey 65
    Chapter 4: The Other Side of the Desk 67
    Chapter 5: Community and Colleagues 85
    Chapter 6: Senior Administration 103

PART THREE: Reflections 151
    Chapter 7: A Life Interwoven 153
    Chapter 8: Passionate Leadership 166
    Chapter 9: Purposeful Leadership 174

AFTERWORD: A Letter to Charles and Isabelle 195

ABOUT THE AUTHOR 217

INTRODUCTION

A Destination and a Journey

The story of my life over the past sixty-five years, from my birth in Lebanon on February 17, 1961, to the present, holds meaning only through the arc of experiences it encompasses and what they may reveal. As biographer Hermione Lee has observed, "There is no such thing as a life lived in isolation." I have come to realize that my own experiences are a form of history and that my viewpoints might be of value. My main motivation for writing this memoir, however, is less lofty: This work is for the benefit of the next generations in my family, both immediate and extended. Becoming a grandparent in 2024 and again in 2026 has increased my desire to share and make meaning of my life's experiences.

Yet motivation is not enough. In 1960, Roy Pascal published a seminal book, *Design and Truth in Autobiography*, in which he offered a traditional contrast between autobiography and memoir: "In the autobiography proper, attention is focused on the self, in the memoir or reminiscence on others." Today, some think that this definition seems antiquated. Subsequently, in 2009, Ben Yagoda claimed in *Memoir: A History* that in the twenty-first century memoir, "attention is resolutely focused on the self, and a certain leeway or looseness with the facts is expected." In the book that follows, however, I adhere resolutely to Pascal's definition, with focus on my experiences as instances of reminiscence that allow me to reflect on my personal and professional journey and perhaps discover insights I may have missed in the moment. I have no interest in factual leeway. My love of tradition allows me to offer a sense of connection, not only for myself but also for others who might find value in my experiences, showing that every story, no matter how personal, holds merit because it is true. In this truth is a way for me to recognize and honor the people who have been there for me in my journey.

I hope that my grandchildren will find in my story purpose, resilience, sacrifice, and love. For them, I write not to impress, but to inspire. I want them to know where they come from, what their family has endured and accomplished, and the values that shaped the life my family and I built together. I wish it to serve both as a personal history and as a message of hope for their own journeys. I especially hope this wish is fulfilled for my grandson Charles Fadi, born to Andrew Deek and Michelle Regna on December 17, 2024, and granddaughter Isabelle Asha, born to Matthew Deek and Nisha Narula on March 5, 2026.

~

I was born in a land rich in culture, family, and tradition yet marked by strife and recurring conflict throughout its long history. During my youth, our country was engulfed in civil war and suffered under prolonged occupation. These were difficult and volatile times. There were days filled with uncertainty, years shadowed by instability. Yet even amid insecurities, our home was grounded in faith, love, and encouragement.

My brothers and I were taught the value of education, integrity, and perseverance. My parents made countless sacrifices for us; sacrifices that, as a child, I could not fully understand but now see clearly. My mother, in particular, shaped me and my brothers in profound ways. She was a woman of quiet strength, sensible wisdom, and limitless love. She taught by example through her actions more than her words, although her sayings and stories were truly precious. She guided us with discipline and grace, even as she shouldered immense burdens with little complaint. Her influence has echoed throughout my life. Even now, her voice still guides me when I face difficult choices.

When the opportunity came to leave my homeland in order to complete my higher education in the United States of America, it was both a leap of faith and an act of survival. I left behind everything familiar—my family, my language, my culture—for the hope of something better. The journey was not easy. Already longing for the familiar, I arrived in America with a heavy heart, overwhelmed by the sadness of leaving home behind and the uncertainty of what lay ahead. My limited English language skills and tight resources made me wonder whether I would ever truly belong here, but I also carried with me dreams, determination, and a sense of responsibility. I knew that I had to succeed, not only for myself but for the family who believed in me and the future they sacrificed so much to make possible.

My college years were a time of intense learning, not only academically but personally. It was also where I met someone who would become the center of my life, from a classmate to a soulmate. Maura, who became my wife and partner in every sense of the word, and I connected over shared values and study sessions that blossomed into love and mutual respect. Our relationship deepened as we supported each other through the challenges of student life, cultural adjustment, and the uncertain future ahead. Together, we imagined a life that would one day include a family, a home, and the chance to give back just as we have been fortunate to receive.

That dream became our unified mission, and eventually a reality. After the completion of our college studies, we worked hard to establish a stable life, even as I pursued advanced degrees and the demanding path of academia. There were long days and longer nights. I spent years learning, teaching, researching, and climbing the academic ladder. I benefited from the support of many people who believed in me when I needed it most. But none of it would have been possible without Maura's unwavering support. My wife balanced, and delayed, her own professional aspirations to do the daily work of raising our children, keeping our home, and anchoring our family through the many transitions and uncertainties that life threw our way. I am deeply grateful for the strength, love, and steady presence she brought to every stage of our lives. Together, we raised three children who are now accomplished professionals in their own right, with advanced degrees and careers in medicine and academia. They are bright, kind, and grounded individuals who carry with them the values we worked so hard to instill. Watching them become the people they are today is one of the greatest rewards of our lives.

~

Charles and Isabelle, your story begins long before you were born. You come from a lineage strong in faith, personal resilience, and cultural richness. You are the continuation of our dreams, hopes, struggles, and realities.

You have inherited more than just a name. You have inherited a history of survival, progress, and love. Lebanon, "the land of milk and honey," is your ancestral homeland. Never forget that. Carry your heritage with pride and step into the future with confidence. Your faith, family, and culture are enduring sources of strength.

Though I will not always be around to guide you, I hope the stories in this book stay with you, even in some small way. Know that your grandfather and grandmother value knowledge, diligence, and family. Know that you can overcome whatever challenges life may place in your path, just as we did.

Know that you are loved beyond measure.

PART ONE

The Destination

My view of the Mediterranean Sea for the first two decades of my life.

CHAPTER 1

Leaving My Homeland

I am one of millions of Lebanese who have left our country, for various reasons. We have established our presence, in many forms, in new lands across the globe.

And so I begin with history.

For Lebanon, outward migration started in 1854, when the first citizen of Mount Lebanon, then a semi-autonomous region under the Ottoman Empire's reign, left for the United States, marking the start of the first wave of emigration. While many left Lebanon to escape religious persecution and conflict, others left in search of economic opportunities or to reunite with family. This impulse to voyage out, perhaps, is in our blood as Phoenicians, ancestors to the Lebanese, who were explorers and seafarers that ventured from their shores in the Levant, bequeathing to the world a lasting legacy of language, trade, geography, and culture. The historical inhabitants of Lebanon have an ancient tradition of exploration beyond their borders. The Phoenicians used their maritime skills to market their commercial goods across the Mediterranean Sea and colonized trade outposts in North Africa and Spain as well as in every major island of the Mediterranean, including Cyprus, Sicily, Malta, Sardinia, and Corsica. Over the centuries, many more emigration waves followed and continue to this day. While some who left Lebanon have returned, including members of my own family, most did not. My fellow voyagers and I have created a visible, active, and accomplished diaspora larger than Lebanon's current population.

~

Geographically, Lebanon is part of the biblical Land of Canaan, which encompassed much of what is now referred to as the Levant, a region rich in cultural, religious, and historical significance. It is also part of the Holy Land, revered across religious traditions of Judaism, Christianity, and Islam. The Levant is the geographic region along the Eastern Mediterranean coast and includes the modern-day countries of Lebanon, Syria, Jordan, Israel, Palestine, Cyprus, as well as parts of Türkiye (i.e., the Hatay Province), Iraq, and Egypt.

The term "Levant" came into existence as early as the fifteenth and sixteenth centuries with the European interest in the region, especially in trade. Gradually, the terminology evolved when the lands just east of Europe came to be known as the Near East, which included Lebanon, while the lands farthest east became the Far East. The Near East encompassed regions geographically broader than the Levant, extending into parts of Iran, the Arabian Peninsula, and North Africa. In the early twentieth century, a new term emerged, the Middle East, referring to this geographic area as well as additional territories further east. Modern Lebanon, with its borders defined in 1920 during the French Mandate period following the First World War, is situated between Israel to its south and Syria to its north and east. Due to its history and geography, Lebanon is a culturally and religiously diverse nation. For centuries, it has been shaped by belief, conquest, famine, war, and occupation. These events have left their mark on Lebanese people, particularly Christians, across generations.

I see myself as an individual shaped by the many cultures, languages, and histories of an ancient land. While some prefer for their affiliation the precision of geography, with borders drawn, I prefer to belong with the infinite variety of people and cultures that have always been there rather than to the lines drawn by circumstances. I am Lebanese. My ancestors are the Canaanites. The Levant is our home.

I have carefully thought and written about this rich history in an earlier book, *The Enduring Presence of Christianity in Lebanon*, which was published in 2025. That book explains the various entities that had conquered Lebanon's predecessor, Canaan, or Phoenicia, and the subsequent spread of Christianity in Lebanon during the reign of the Roman and Byzantine empires. It also discusses the conquests from the Arabian Peninsula, the spread of Islam and arrival of the Arabic language to the Levant, the ensuing Crusades to the Holy Land, and the return of more Muslim conquests. I discuss the First World War, the formation of modern Lebanon, and the impact of all this on Christians—resulting in the death of many and the migration out of Lebanon for many others. The book concludes with a reflection on the patterns and consequences of past events and decisions as a means to understanding the present and perhaps informing the future. In addition, I offer a set of recommendations, along with a new identity, for an inclusive and prosperous Lebanon.

Together, *The Enduring Presence of Christianity in Lebanon* and *Portrait of an Expatriate* form a documentary that intertwines my personal history with the religious and cultural history of Lebanon, offering a unique perspective on both individual and collective identity. Seen another way, this memoir tells the backstory of history.

~

Even though I had already finished three years of a college curriculum focusing on the applied study of electronics while still living in Lebanon, I chose to leave and complete my higher education in the United States. For generations, and despite Lebanon having strong public and private higher education systems, a considerable number of students pursued their studies abroad. Traditionally, most went to Europe, particularly France, largely because of linguistic convenience, as French was the primary foreign language taught in Lebanon. My own decision and timing were shaped by several factors: the intensifying of the Civil War from 1975 to 1990, the perceived advantages of earning an international degree, and, specifically, the growing importance of an American education as a valuable professional edge.

In my generation, I was not the only one to leave for reasons similar to mine. In fact, for decades before I left, it had been common for the Lebanese to seek trade, professional, or higher education opportunities abroad and return with financial assets, knowledge and skills, or academic degrees, resources that were instrumental in propelling Lebanon into economic prosperity. Legacies in education, commerce, science, medicine, the arts, entertainment, and politics all contributed to making our modern Lebanese society vibrant and our culture progressive. Descending into recurring and lasting cycles of violence, beginning in 1975, has made our beautiful homeland perilous, eventually culminating in its total social and financial collapse.

~

Given its many layers of history, Lebanon is like a living museum. It is often described as having breathtaking beauty, with lush flora and fauna. From its stunning Mediterranean coastline to its rugged mountains and fertile valleys, this small, geographically diverse country is often used in poetic and prophetic imagery. Ancient Lebanon is referenced repeatedly in the Old Testament to demonstrate the beauty of God's magnificent creation, most notably its famous cedar forests. These forests were celebrated for their grandeur, strength, and purity, and came to symbolize majesty and resilience in biblical literature.

Every corner of the country seems to have a story to tell. The contrast between the mountains and the sea is striking. In addition to majestic views and hiking spots, the snow-covered slopes offer great skiing in winter. And, in between the mountain ranges, there is the Beqaa Valley, known for its vast agricultural land and vineyards. The valley is also home to the impressive Baalbek ruins, where the colossal temple of Jupiter, one of the largest ever built, stands. The same site also houses the temples of Bacchus and Venus, smaller but equally impressive structures. In summer, the Mediterranean beaches offer a blend of swimming and high energy water sports. Living there for the first two decades of my life, practically on the beach and in proximity to the mountains, I enjoyed both the peaceful escape of swimming and the serene beauty of skiing.

Living in a melting pot of cultures and religions, the Lebanese people are known for their warmth, hospitality, and pride in their heritage. Even with their turbulent history and continuing uncertainties, they have always shown resilience and vibrancy especially in the arts, culture, and cuisine. Lebanese art thrives in fashionable galleries and in city and town squares. Beirut, in particular, has always been a cultural hub, where one can appreciate contemporary art and marvel at ancient artifacts or sit at a café and sip dark-roast Arabica coffee in a city that blends old-world charm with modern design. The city's architecture, inspired by a blend of Roman, Arab, Mamluk, Ottoman, and French colonial flair, exists in harmony with the more contemporary structures built after our 1943 independence from the French.

Food is central to Lebanese life and reflects the country's focus on family and togetherness. Our baba ghanoush, kibbeh, and falafel are world renowned, made out of ingredients that are always fresh, flavorful, and healthy. The baklava dessert, every taste of it, is heavenly. Although unusual for a boy growing up in Lebanon, I was my mother's helper in the kitchen, especially on Sundays and during the period of holidays. This training has paid handsome dividends for me when I found myself on my own, and for members of my family who love our Lebanese cuisine.

Music is also an essential part of life, blending traditional stringed instruments like the oud and buzuq, woodwinds like the mijwiz and ney, and percussion instruments like the tabla and daf, with Western instruments like the piano, guitar, and violin. For many decades, famed music festivals, including the Byblos International Festival, the Cedars International Festival, the Baalbek International Festival, and the Beiteddine International Festival brought together Lebanese and international artists for performances that delighted the local population and visiting tourists. Attending the events of the Byblos International Festival, just a short stroll from where I lived, was the highlight of my summers.

Along the entire coast, Lebanon's Phoenician cities are filled with historical treasures that reflect the country's rich cultural layers. In some of the oldest cities in the world—Tripoli, Batroun, Byblos, Beirut, Sidon, and Tyre—ancient ruins exist side by side with the conveniences of modern life. And, then there is one of the most impressive natural wonders of the world, the Jeita Grotto, a series of caves that is home to an underground river, stalactites, and stalagmites that create an eerie otherworldly atmosphere. The Grotto is tucked away beneath Mount Lebanon in the valley of Nahr al-Kalb, or Dog River, ten miles north of Beirut, and only about a hundred meters above sea level. The beauty within is the result of millions of years of water slowly and persistently shaping limestone into incredible formations. I have fond memories of visiting every one of these locations, some many times. I still remember as a young child my father hiring a taxi driver on some Sundays during our summer breaks to visit the monuments and attractions in these cities. The Jeita Grotto was a favorite spot for my family to visit.

~

I am not the only member of my immediate family who left Lebanon. On my father's side, my great-grandfather, Joseph Bechara Deek and great-grandmother, Elisabeth Deek, emigrated to France from the Sidon area in the early 1900s, traveling through North Africa while the region was still under the Ottomans' rule. My grandfather, Wadih, one of six children, Lebanese through his father's lineage, was born in Tunisia in 1905, during a lengthy stopover as his family made their way to France.

Eventually, most of my grandfather's family settled in France, but some of the Deeks ended up back in Lebanon after the end of the First World War. My grandfather himself returned a decade after the 1920 proclamation of Grand Liban by the French, in an official capacity as a French citizen and an officer of the Division Navale Du Levant (Naval Division of the Levant). He was twenty-five years old. He remained in service until 1941. His final title in the Naval Division of the Levant was Chief of Police for the Beirut Barrack. Like many others who served in the French army there, my grandfather remained in Lebanon subsequent to the war's conclusion for a number of reasons, including that the commanders of these troops had aligned themselves with Vichy France, the losing side.

After the fall of France in 1940, the Vichy government, in collaboration with Nazi Germany, took control of the French overseas territories, including Lebanon. The French troops stationed in Lebanon became aligned with the Central Powers, alongside Germany, Austria-Hungary, and later, Bulgaria, and fought against the Allied Powers of Great Britain, France, Italy, Russia, and Japan, with the United States subsequently joining in. When the Central

Powers were defeated, they handed control to the victorious Free French government.

My paternal grandfather in front of the Naval Division of the Levant Barrack in Beirut.

My grandmother on my father's side, Melani BouZeid, was born in Cuba in 1906. Her parents, Habib BouZeid and Fahta Abboud, had also emigrated from the Sidon region to escape Ottoman rule. Their return to Lebanon after the war marked the beginning of a new chapter, one that would eventually allow my father, the eldest of five children, and his siblings to grow up in the land his grandparents had once fled.

~

My great-grandfather on my mother's side, Khalil Nader, emigrated to Brazil at the age of seventeen, from the area of Jbeil, also known by its Greek name of Byblos, during the era of Ottoman rule. After seven years abroad, he returned to Lebanon to marry Mariam Bilan, the daughter of a wealthy landowner from Jbeil, and left again for Brazil in 1907. The Naders too ended up returning to Lebanon permanently, arriving just a short while before the First World War started. Their return was made possible by the significant savings they accumulated in Brazil. They were also drawn back by the desire of my great-grandmother's wealthy parents. Immediately after the conclusion of the war, my great-grandfather became involved in local politics and served for a long time as mayor of his hometown. Also, Khalil Nader became a respected and successful merchant in Jbeil, enabled by the renewed hope for peace and prosperity brought on by the emerging new Lebanese society under the French Mandate for Lebanon that began in 1918. The Naders had twelve children. Rosa, my grandmother, was born in 1912.

Rosa married my grandfather, Zakhia Nakhle, a farmer, also from the area of Jbeil, who was born in Lebanon in 1908, a decade before the end of the Ottomans' rule in 1918. After the death of his father at a young age, he was raised by his mother alone, and they lived through the hardships of the First World War. My grandfather was the only child in his family to survive the famine that struck Lebanon during the war, precipitated by the harsh land control measures put in place by the Ottoman rulers that cut off food supplies to the local population. Disease, periods of drought, and severe locust infestation further aggravated the situation.

With my maternal grandfather on his farm in 1993. He
worked the land from when he was a young boy, during the
First World War, until shortly before his passing.

The Ottomans' four-hundred-year reign of Mount Lebanon, starting in 1516, can be described as a period of hardship of varying intensity, fluctuating based on both external and internal factors. They were the last of the successive Muslim Caliphates, starting in 636, that ruled the Levant, and therefore Mount Lebanon. The Ottomans allowed communities within their sphere to manage their own local affairs based on religious affiliation, called the millet system, while remaining subordinate to the supremacy of the Ottoman administration. Out of necessity, starting in the early part of the nineteenth century, the inhabitants of Mount Lebanon, at the time made up of a Christian majority and a Druze minority, were given increased autonomy. They were still overseen by the

Ottoman hierarchy, but with the assistance of local proxies who controlled the land and handled taxation on behalf of the Ottomans.

For the most part, the two religious communities of Mount Lebanon went about their daily lives separately, but peacefully. However, there were occasional violent clashes between the two, requiring the intervention of Ottoman authority to suppress them. The Ottomans were not always successful in resolving all disputes and, in fact, at times purposefully fanned them into violent sectarian discords to justify their own interference. There are two noteworthy conflicts; one was in 1840 and the other in 1860. Both reached dangerous levels, leading to massacres and destruction in both the Christian and Druze communities. As a result of these events, Mount Lebanon was re-placed under strict direct rule of Ottoman authority, putting in place new measures to centralize power and reduce the influence of local rule. This period marked the beginning of the Lebanese Christian emigration to the West, with the first person arriving in the United States in 1854. Many more departures out of Mount Lebanon followed, as Christians fled violence, heavy taxation, and conscription into the Ottomans' armed forces. The waves of migration further intensified in the decades leading up to and following the First World War. This history is necessary to understand that the sea and land blockade put in place by the Ottoman rulers during the war was emblematic of the oppression Lebanon faced.

The war years were devastating for many Mount Lebanon families, including my own, especially due to the desperate and extreme measures taken by the Ottomans to enforce their dominance, including the burning of harvests and the hanging of Lebanese who were active in freedom movements. A 1915 drought and a locust infestation decimated Mount Lebanon's agricultural base and exacerbated the situation. The Ottoman military, concerned with the impact of food scarcity on its own forces, imposed stringent controls on the sale and transport of essential grains such as wheat and barley. These measures aggravated the dire food shortages, transforming the crisis into a full-blown famine that lasted until the end of the war in 1918. Diseases spread rapidly among the population. Naval blockades in the Eastern Mediterranean, enforced by both sides of the warring powers, prevented any form of aid from arriving in Mount Lebanon and its coastal region. The suffering, starvation, and death that ensued became a grim daily reality for many in Lebanon. Anyone who had the means to leave did; with deaths and emigration, Mount Lebanon nearly emptied.

The Ottoman Caliphate collapsed in 1918, and Lebanon was placed under the League of Nations' French Mandate. Aspirations for an independent Lebanon became a reality at the 1919 Paris Peace Conference. A year later, in 1920, the state of Greater Lebanon was proclaimed by the French.

Even under these dire circumstances, my grandfather chose to remain by his mother's side. When a maternal uncle who had left Lebanon for Brazil a year before the start of the war offered to bring him there after the war began, he declined. Of my grandparents' nine children, two died in early childhood. My mother was the third oldest among those who survived.

~

The fall of the Ottoman Empire, the last of a series of Caliphates that ruled Lebanon and the Levant starting in 636 during the time of the Byzantine Empire and ending in 1918, ushered in a new era for Lebanon. The "interwar period" under French rule, approximately the twenty years between the end of the First World War and the start of the Second World War, was highly influential in establishing a civic and modern society in Lebanon modeled after Western systems. This period brought Lebanon to the forefront of economies in the Levant, despite its small size compared to its neighboring nations.

During this period of prosperity, my father, Pierre Deek, was born on February 5, 1935—a mere fifteen years after the establishment of *État du Grand Liban* by the French. My mother, Maria Thérèse Deek, was born on April 25, 1938—five years before the unwritten National Pact that ensured the representation of different Christian and Muslim religious communities in the Lebanese government.

The Second World War, from 1939 to 1945, placed the country in proximity to armed conflict, with French troops stationed in Lebanon becoming loyal to the Vichy government that was collaborating closely with Germany. However, it also brought independence from France in 1943 after Free French troops arrived in Lebanon and defeated the Vichy French forces. The remaining French troops withdrew in 1946. As expected, the hostilities and economic ramifications of the war prompted another significant wave of emigration from Lebanon.

However, an opulent span that we may refer to as the Golden Modern Age followed the Second World War and independence. Lebanon experienced a period of economic growth, cultural renaissance, and political stability resulting from its favorable position as a liberal society and a regional center for education, culture, finance, and tourism. Beirut emerged as a hub for intellectual exchange with a vibrant scene in literature, arts, theater, and music. The country's power-sharing political system ensured relative peace, attracting a significant presence of multi-national corporations, while Lebanon's universities attracted students from across the world. Lebanon was peaceful and prosperous, for a while.

~

Born into a farming family, my mother, Maria Thérèse Nakhle-Deek, received limited formal education. She first studied basic literacy and numeracy skills as well as Syriac, a dialect of Aramaic, the language of the Maronite Church of Antioch, in Edde, a small town overlooking the city of Jbeil, from the town priest, Father Youssef. She completed her elementary education at the Saint Joseph School of the Maronite Sisters of the Holy Family in Jbeil, where one of her maternal aunts, Amalia Nader, was a teacher.

My mother and father met on her father's farm when my father moved from Beirut in 1958, during a significant period of political crisis and armed conflict in Lebanon, to take a new job as an agricultural consultant working for Lebanon's national tobacco company, consistent with his education at Beirut's school of agriculture. The company was initially established in 1935 under the French Mandate rules to operate and oversee all aspects of tobacco in Lebanon, from agriculture to manufacturing and from marketing to distribution. He was assigned to the district of Jbeil. They were married in the same year, and together they lovingly raised five boys, one of whom predeceased my mother. She was a dedicated mother to her children and a support to many in her immediate and extended family, as well as to her friends.

Life was eventful for my parents with the defining moment coming too early in their lives together, with lasting ramifications for everyone in their household. Within six months of my parents' marriage, my father was involved in a hunting accident that would quietly shape the rest of his and my mother's lives, and the lives of all of us who came after. He was twenty-three years old. While hunting on my maternal grandparents' farm on the hills above the city of Jbeil, his own rifle backfired due to a defective capsule in the back of the cartridge he was using. The resulting explosion caused a severe injury to his head. He was transported to a hospital in Beirut, Hôtel-Dieu de France, some twenty-five miles away. Remarkably, on the way, despite the seriousness of his injury and the heavy bleeding, he was conscious enough to remove the cartridge that had backfired into his forehead with his own fingers. At the hospital, doctors focused on saving his life. His wounds were cleaned, bandaged, and treated. After a long hospital stay, and the excellent care he received, my father slowly recovered. In the process, however, the defective capsule itself was not detected and remained lodged in his head.

My father was released from the hospital on the very day his first child, my older brother, Wadih, was born. Pregnant and slowly approaching her due date, my mother remained with my father at the hospital from the day of the accident until hours before her delivery, when she was taken to the nearby Trad Maternity Hospital to give birth. It took time for my father to recover fully, but eventually he was able to return to an active life. For several years, it seemed as though the worst was behind him. However, nine years later, an infection developed, caused by the capsule left behind for all those years. Decades of pain for my father and those who loved him followed. But one important fact was confirmed. When the accident first happened, my paternal grandparents refused to believe the story that my father's injury was caused by a hunting accident; they insisted that their son was purposely shot, causing lingering tension with my mother and her family. Now that the ill-fated capsule was found resting on my father's frontal lobe, this mystery was solved.

By then, I was six years old, the second of four children, with one older and two younger brothers. Over the next decade, my father underwent a total of four operations to address both the original cause of the injury and the many complications resulting from it. There were long stretches of hospitalization, and medical care became a constant presence in our lives. For us children, it was a confusing and frightening time. We obviously did not understand the medical details, but we felt the seriousness of the situation and the interruptions to normal life. Our father was there, but not always well, and our world felt fragile. The loss of a substantial amount of bone density in his forehead, leaving a visibly large area protected only by skin, was a constant reminder of all this.

For my mother, the years were especially hard. She took care of my father's needs and the needs of her five, yes, five, boys. My mother was pregnant with our youngest brother, Roland, when my father learned that he had redeveloped an infection related to his old injury. My father's drinking habits worsened, becoming a daily routine. Though alcohol did help him with the constant pain, as he justified it, it also created tension in our home. He also smoked heavily, perhaps explaining his subsequent quadruple bypass surgery, and then a further corrective bypass surgery a short while after. While heavy smoking was not unusual for my parents' generation at that time, watching my father cope with chronic pain through excessive drinking was unsettling for me, and I am certain for my brothers, especially in how this affected our father's overall health and behavior. That we were aware of the financial toll our family was under resulting from medical-related expenses added to the emotional unpredictability, sadness, and fear we experienced for my father's pain. Throughout it all, my mother's role was nothing short of heroic. She provided stability during years marked by medical crises and uncertainty. Her strength became the quiet foundation on which all of us depended.

My mother assumed responsibility and exhibited wisdom from an early age. Access to medical services was scarce in the farming community where she lived when she was a young girl. When her father fell ill and needed ongoing care, she learned how to give injections by watching the doctor treat him so she could help her father with the rest of his medical regimen and avoid expensive house call visits. This was a skill that remained with her, and one which she generously volunteered, using it extensively to help others well into her older years.

My mother never worked outside the home. As a wife and a mother, her role was an incredible vow of self-sacrifice, patience, commitment, and endurance as she tenderly focused on the up-bringing of her boys, their well-being, schooling, and anything else imaginable. Her life as a spouse was complicated by the necessity to devote special attention to the needs of our father. Thérèse remained a dedicated wife to Pierre, her husband of fifty-three years, until he passed in 2011.

~

From an early age, I understood the value of commitment and dedication through my mother's example. Not because my brothers or I experienced many challenges. In fact, our parents made the sacrifices in sending us to private schools in Lebanon and then abroad for college so that we could obtain the best education possible. Instead, it was the occasional story from my mother's own childhood, how she could only attend school on days when it rained because on sunny days she had to work on her father's farm, that had an impact on me. At the time, it seemed my mother was merely recounting her life experiences. Yet hearing her stories in comparison to my own childhood, and now thinking about the life Charles and Isabelle will live, made me realize the consequences of dedicated work.

A meaningful line from the New Testament—"By their fruit you will recognize them" (Matthew 7:16-20)—seems to have guided my mother in setting her family's priorities. It was paramount for her that her children know, appreciate, and receive the blessings of a compassionate and gracious God. Beyond praying, the simple practices of everyday life made the priorities always clear. Respect for others and personal responsibility led her attitude towards the world. My mother was also passionate about responsibility to country and was always proud of the social and political activism undertaken by all her children, in various forms and at different stages of their lives, on behalf of Lebanon's freedom, sovereignty, and independence. Within the family, education was the gateway to success for her sons. As youngsters, my mother's decree filled our lives: "Studying is next to praying."

When the opportunity presented itself, my mother managed to impact the lives of children other than hers as well. As we grew older and four of us left Lebanon to pursue higher education opportunities, she found time for community service as a volunteer teacher of Christian Catechism at public schools in Jbeil and nearby towns for fifteen years. Indeed, my mother was devout, but most importantly, she lived the faith she believed.

Receiving my Holy Eucharist for the first time.

~

My mother was a sensible woman, witty and philosophical, and her children were beneficiaries of her intuition. "She opens her mouth with wisdom, and the teaching of kindness is on her tongue" (Proverbs 31:26). This verse reveals how my mother's ordinary words came across. She was always able to say things that were rational, wise, and captured the essence of a situation or circumstance, a trait she inherited from her father.

I was one of five boys, the second oldest, and although we were all very different, my parents loved us equally. This led to one of my mother's most cherished sayings: "You are like my hand. It has five fingers; none are alike; they have different heights, sizes, and traits, but my hand looks perfect as is." A very early lesson on differences and equality!

My mother's words carried lessons that resonated with all of us but also far beyond the walls of our family home. In reflecting on them, I see a simple yet powerful metaphor that encapsulates truths about the beauty of individuality. As five brothers, close to each other in age but each unique in our own way, her simile became a guiding principle in our lives, teaching us to respect and appreciate our differences while recognizing the strength of our unity. From these words, we drew invaluable lessons about love, acceptance, harmony, and the importance of seeing the bigger picture.

At its core, my mother's metaphor both heightened and celebrated our differences. Just as the five fingers of a hand are distinct in their shape, size, and function, so too are the members of our family—really any other family or group of individuals. My brothers and I typified this perfectly. I witnessed firsthand how our personalities, interests, and talents varied widely. One of us was laid-back and carefree; another was logical and patient; one was athletic and competitive; another was funny and outgoing; yet another was determined and focused. Despite these differences, my parents loved us equally, never favoring one over the other. Their unconditional love taught us that our individuality was not a source of division but a complement. In a world that often pressures people to conform, my mother's words remind us that diversity is not a flaw but a strength. It is what makes us unique and contributes to the richness of our collective experience.

The image of the hand, with each finger being distinct, also underscores the importance of equality. My mother's saying emphasized that while we were different, we were equally valued and loved. This lesson reaches beyond the family unit to broader societal contexts. As inequality and discrimination persist in our world, my mother's words serve as a poignant reminder that every individual, regardless of their background, abilities, or beliefs, deserves respect and dignity. Just as a hand cannot function properly if one finger is missing, a community or society cannot thrive if any groups are excluded. Equality does not mean treating everyone the same; it means recognizing and acknowledging the inherent worth of each person, ensuring that everyone has the opportunity to participate and prosper.

Thinking back on my relationship with my brothers, *Five in One* is the brand we might call ourselves in today's terms. It demonstrated that our differences were not obstacles but assets, each of us bringing something that forms a unique whole. This lesson is particularly relevant in today's interconnected world, where global challenges require collective actions and diverse perspectives. By valuing and leveraging our differences, we are stronger and more resilient.

My mother's saying also carries a subtle yet profound message about perspective. To the casual observer, a hand with fingers of varying lengths and shapes might seem imperfect. Yet, to my mother, that hand was *perfect as is*. This sense of completeness reflects a truth about beauty and perfection: they are not absolute but subjective. What one person might see as a flaw, another might see as a source of strength or uniqueness. This lesson compels us to readjust our perspective, to look beyond superficial judgments and appreciate distinctiveness. It challenges us to redefine our standards of perfection, recognizing that true beauty lies in authenticity and the harmonious coexistence of differences. "You are like my hand" is far more than just a saying, or a family motto; it is a profound lesson in equality, unity, and love. It challenges us to see the beauty in imperfection and to recognize the strength that comes from collaboration and mutual respect. It reminds us that our differences are not something to be feared but accepted and embraced. Most importantly, this lesson teaches us that acceptance is an essential foundation for any strong relationship, whether in a family or a community.

Ultimately, my mother taught us about the power of love. Her unwavering devotion for her five sons, despite our differences, created a foundation of security and belonging. This love was not conditional on our achievements or conformity but the simple fact that we were her children. In a world that often measures worth by external standards, this unconditional acceptance is a powerful example of the transformative power of love. It shows us that when we love and accept others for who they are, we create an environment where everyone can thrive and reach their full potential. I like to believe that as we navigate the complexities of life, these lessons learned in childhood remain with us, in a world where everyone is valued for who they are, and where our collective differences, just like the five fingers of a hand, make us stronger.

Although my mother and I always shared a wonderful relationship, it was only after her loss that I began to reflect on the many lessons she instilled in me—through her actions, sayings, and personal stories. I can now see much more clearly the influence of my mother's wisdom in my approach to life. Her sayings laid a moral foundation, rules for how to act and how to react, that continue to guide me. In particular, my mother's values and wisdom have been instrumental in my own development as a person and a professional, and I offer those that worked for me, whether a strategy or a perspective, perhaps as a benefit that can help others on their own path.

As I reflect now on my childhood with my four brothers—Wadih Deek, born on August 3, 1959; Bassam Deek, April 6, 1962; Sami Deek, February 5, 1964; and Roland Deek, May 21, 1968—I think of a normal and safe period in our nation's history. During this time, my family—and in fact many, but not all, in Lebanese society—benefited from the cosmopolitan lifestyle and modern education and socioeconomic and political systems that were the envy of the region. Lebanon's multilingual, multicultural talent base was a model for many nations to emulate. Unbeknownst to us, though not a total surprise in retrospect, much of this would begin to unravel starting in the late 1960s, reaching a boiling point in the mid-1970s, with the emergence of foreign armed groups on Lebanese soil challenging its authority.

Our world was perfect. Until it was not.

~

On April 13, 1975, that world of peace and prosperity ended. Violence erupted outside the Church of our Lady of Deliverance in Ain el-Remmaneh, a suburb of Beirut, marking the beginning of the Lebanese Civil War. The seeds of this prolonged conflict had been sown generations before.

During the 1970s, Lebanon became a battleground for regional and international powers. The Palestinian presence in Lebanon, which started with a significant influx following the initial Arab-Israeli War of 1948 and continued through the Arab-Israeli War of 1967 and the Palestinian-Jordanian War of 1970, played a pivotal role in escalating tensions and sparking the Lebanese Civil War. The Palestine Liberation Organization's armed activities in South Lebanon and Beirut, along with their ongoing conflict with Israel on Lebanese soil, heightened tensions between them and Lebanese citizens, specifically among the Christians. This war was a complex and multifaceted conflict that had far-reaching consequences for Lebanon and the broader region. It was not a single war but rather a series of interconnected conflicts involving a variety of political, sectarian, and external factors. Other countries, global and regional, became involved either directly or through proxy groups.

As a tiny nation of a little over 4,000 square miles, the entire country was impacted by the brutality of war, in one way or another. While the actual fighting initially started in a suburb of Beirut, situated in the center of the country, closer to its Mediterranean coast, it quickly spread in all directions. Fear and uncertainty loomed constantly as individuals and families faced the ever-present threat of violence, especially the random type, whether it was bombings, gunfire, kidnappings, or attacks by armed groups. Basic needs like power, clean water, and food became scarce. Education, at all levels, was severely disrupted. Access to medical care deteriorated and psychological trauma became widespread.

A large number of people living in dangerous areas left their homes to escape the fighting, or were forcefully displaced, losing their livelihoods, and, for many, their lives, in the process. Families were frequently separated, with different members fleeing in different directions. Most members of my family, particularly on my father's side, lived in Beirut and other parts of the country facing hostilities. We hosted them in our home, often multiple families at a time, until they were able to secure new living arrangements in safer areas. Many of them became permanently displaced from their original homes. Ultimately, the war systematically eroded the central capabilities for a dignified life, undermining human worth, restricting freedoms, suppressing rights, and impacting the overall well-being of a large segment of the Lebanese population.

For me and others in my generation, the ability to plan for the future seemed impossible. Instead, we had to prioritize decisions about how best to navigate the commute to school, college, or work along the paths least prone to shelling, how to dodge sniper fire at crossroads, and how to stay clear of car bombs. With no end in sight for the war and with the future uncertain, the thought of emigration first crossed my mind after I completed high school, in 1979, but I was still committed to a future in Lebanon.

The war lasted for fifteen years, much longer in reality, and was devastating for Lebanon, reshaping its political and social landscape. By 1990, after much destruction and bloodshed, a peace accord, the Taif Agreement, was negotiated in 1989 in Saudi Arabia and ratified by the Lebanese government, bringing an end to the war. The agreement restructured the Lebanese political system, redistributing power to Muslims, a shift justified by evolving demographics, while keeping Christians, increasingly marginalized, in diminished key positions. After the war ended, Lebanon faced a long and difficult recovery process that is nowhere near completion as I write this memoir.

The Taif Agreement, along with subsequent constitutional amendments, changed many elements of material life in Lebanese society including sociopolitical influence among the different groups in the country. In an unbearable loss resulting from the Civil War, an estimated 150,000 people were killed, with another 200,000 injured or permanently disabled. More than one million, roughly a quarter of the population, were internally displaced from their homes, with many villages completely destroyed to this day. Another quarter of the Lebanese population emigrated, leaving the country altogether. Lebanon's total population in 1990 was 3.5 million, inclusive of the relatively large cohort of non-citizens living in the country, with Palestinians being the majority among them.

One of the legacies of the Civil War is Lebanon's enduring sectarian political system, which often paralyzes governance. Although the early form of such a system was put in place and has been in practice since the mid 1800s, under the Ottomans, it is now affirmed in the Lebanese constitution. The Taif Agreement sought to balance the interests of all religious groups, but it has entrenched the divide and is widely seen as a major obstacle to long-term stability and reform. Meanwhile, today the country remains mired in political, economic, and social challenges. Despite the end of the Civil War, many of its root causes—sectarianism, external interference, and regional conflicts—remain unresolved. The legacy of the war, particularly the fractured political structure and ongoing instability, continues to shape the country's uncertain path forward.

~

I had already left Lebanon by the time the Civil War ended, at least officially. For me, a pivotal moment was midway through the war. With multiple foreign forces occupying Lebanon and the violence at its peak, I realized that I would soon become one of the Lebanese citizens to emigrate. I remember the exact day of my decision: September 14, 1982. Bachir Gemayel, the president-elect of Lebanon, was assassinated on that day in a bombing at his headquarters in Beirut, twenty-two days after his election, at the age of thirty-four. Prior to his election, he was a prominent political activist and the leader of the Lebanese resistance against foreign armed forces working to destabilize the state, specifically Palestinian and Syrian forces. President-elect Gemayel's assassination was a major shock, not only because of his prominence, but also because of the way his death quickly intensified the ongoing conflict. The assassination became a pivotal moment in Lebanon's history, ending what many hoped would be a new era of stability under his leadership and throwing Lebanon into even more turmoil.

I had been active in student politics, including in the Lebanese resistance, since my high school days and through the early stages of college in Lebanon, and I began to realize that the dream of a strong government and a democratic, sovereign state had passed. I started to question not only the future of my country, but my own future within it.

Growing up in a middle-class family in Lebanon, my childhood was one of stability, support, and the promise of a bright future. I had access to good schools, surrounded myself with friends, and was socially active. However, everything shifted dramatically with the beginning of the war when I was fourteen. I was still in middle school. At first, the war seemed distant. It was localized to an area of Beirut a little more than twenty miles away from where I lived, but in a small country, this distance was significant. Despite this, we were able to continue our daily lives, attending school and engaging in normal activities, but as the war spread, slowly engulfing more regions, the entire country seemed affected by it. So was I. It was not just a passive awareness of the war. I could see and feel what was at stake for our culture, our way of life, and our land.

Literally witnessing the destruction of my homeland, I began to understand that the war threatening my country was instigated by external forces. These were people we had welcomed to our country as refugees, now playing a role in the escalating violence. To be fair, there were also glaring internal divisions. As I entered high school, a sense of nationalism led me to become politically active. I sought to speak out, to organize, and to influence the political debate in my schools. I also became involved in policy advocacy. At the invitation of my friend Raphael Sfeir, I joined a small group of activists he was working with, led by his law school classmate Walid Phares. The aim was to raise awareness about threats to our country's sovereignty. We produced press releases and position papers that we shared with news organizations, especially international media outlets, in order to amplify our perspective globally. Next, I began to engage in debates and discussions, fully immersed in a new world that demanded my attention, propelling me toward leadership positions in student and media divisions of political organizations while in both high school and college. My country was at war, and I was determined to stand up for what I believed was right. Looking back, I realize how impactful that time was for me, a period of growing up quickly and transitioning from the optimism of childhood to the reality and uncertainty of adulthood, in a complex society. I also believe that it was then, during such difficult times, that I acquired my early lessons in leadership, developing new skills in empathy, critical thinking, and the ability to negotiate opposing viewpoints.

With my commitment to societal causes, I became more intellectually curious. I was not at all drawn to the popular sports that my brothers and many of my friends loved and played. While they were engrossed in volleyball, basketball, or other such team sports, I found my own comfort in activities that did not require large groups or competitive teams. I was not as talented as they were in these sports, so attending their games was sufficient for me. My interests leaned more toward individual activities that allowed for reflection and tranquility—like reading.

When I was about thirteen, the arrival of a new priest in my parish, Father Louis Khalife, who served from 1974 to 1981, marked a transformative moment for our community and for me. He had studied and served in a number of parishes in Europe before he was transferred back to Lebanon, bringing with him new ideas and approaches. One of the first things he did was to convert a large hall in the parish center into a public library, which Jbeil had never had before. It quickly became a hub for local youth, providing us a place to study and socialize. My brothers and I spent much of our after-school time there doing our homework. To my delight, I was also able to read nearly every newspaper published in Lebanon, which is how I was informed about what was happening in our country, especially regarding the war. There in that hall, my eyes were opened to encyclopedias, of all sorts, and many reference books on nearly every topic. I remember that I always gravitated toward the history section. Using my allowance, I began to create my own personal library, which remained in my parents' home after my departure to the United States.

I built a modest library, from scratch, with a clear purpose based on my interest in reading. To do this, I was able to access a wide range of book genres at book fairs. Even during the difficult war years, Beirut hosted a number of international and regional literary festivals, which I often attended with my friend Khalil Basil who shared my quest for knowledge. My primary interest was culture and heritage, focusing on Lebanon's history and identity.

My favorite author was Kamal Salibi, who was a professor of history and archeology at the American University of Beirut from 1953 to 1998. He is considered among the most eminent historians of Lebanon, covering both ancient and modern times, including the civil war. My interest in his work began before I understood his prominence. As one of the closest friends of my uncle, Paul Deek, Dr. Salibi routinely joined our holiday meals at my grandparents' home in Beirut. I vividly remember sitting at the dinner table, listening to his passionate narration of the past and connecting it to the present—pulling in politics, culture, religion, and migration. Soon after they were published, early in the war years while I still lived in Lebanon, I obtained and read two of his books focusing on contemporary Lebanese history, *The Modern History of Lebanon* and *Crossroads to Civil War: Lebanon 1958-1976*. These books and my desire to further explore my heritage led me to the work of another eminent and prolific scholar, Philip Hitti, an authority on the Levant's history. A Lebanese-American, Dr. Hitti was a professor of Oriental Languages, Literatures, and Near Eastern Studies at Princeton University from 1926 until 1954. Published in the 1960s, two of his books in particular—*The Near East in History: A 5000-Year Story* and *Lebanon in History: From the Earliest Times to the Present*—provided me deeper understanding of ancient Lebanon and the Levant. Written primarily in Arabic, but also translated to other languages, I admire the works of these two brilliant historians despite their opposing views on Lebanon's past. Dr. Salibi highlights the sectarian divisions and internal social dynamics that have shaped the modern Lebanese society, while Dr. Hitti emphasizes Lebanon's Phoenician roots and its broader connections to the ancient Mediterranean world. For me during that time, both were essential to understanding the complex mosaic of my home.

No Lebanese library is complete without a section on literature and poetry highlighted through some of the county's most famous writers. Lebanese-American Khalil Gibran is someone very special for all of us. He was born in Lebanon, but his family emigrated to the United States when he was young. He later returned to Lebanon as a teenager and continued his education there before coming back to the United States. This internationalism enabled him to write in both Arabic and English, representing his local Lebanese identity and his global American culture. Some of Gibran's books were required readings in our schools. I read *The Broken Wings* and *A Tear and a Smile*, both originally written in Arabic, at a young age. I later read *The Prophet*, twice. I first read a translated version in Arabic in Lebanon, and then I read the original version in English after I came to the United States. With time, I obtained more of his other books, creating a large presence of his works in my library. Gibran's words are simple to understand, yet worthy of reflection for a lifetime. I have found myself returning to him at different stages of my life and finding something new each time.

My interest in politics and policy led me to Beit-al-Mustaqbal, or the House of the Future, a think tank and research center established in 1975, when Lebanon was on the brink of its civil war, to advocate for Lebanese sovereignty given the mounting political tensions in Lebanon and the rising Palestinian military presence, and the historically significant Syrian meddling in the country. The founder of this center, Amin Gemayel, was a prominent Lebanese politician who later became president of Lebanon from 1982 to 1988. I subscribed to Beit-al-Mustaqbal's main publication, *Haliyyat*, a quarterly journal published in Arabic, French, and English. It encompassed a chronology of political events in Lebanon and the region, research essays, and policy reports. *Haliyyat* also published transcripts of panels and working groups of noted public figures and academicians promoting a new direction for Lebanon aiming to resolve the growing divisions between Lebanon's sectarian communities.

I also was interested in reading comparative religion books that explained basic beliefs of Judaism, Christianity, Islam, and other traditions. My desire was not to promote certain religious or cultural practices but rather to understand the similarities and differences between them. I was especially curious to learn how these different communities developed, how they lived side by side over time, and how they diverged to the point of acrimony and war. This is explained so well in the *Al-Muqaddimah*, or *Prolegomena*, a book written by the historian Ibn Khaldun in 1377, in which he presented his view on universal history. It is a very long book, and I read it selectively with an intent to understand the coexistence, divergence, and conflict among these three Abrahamic communities. Ibn Khaldun asserts in the *Al-Muqaddimah* that religious communities do not clash just because of beliefs. Rather, they do so when social, political, and economic structures make conflict more likely than coexistence. And so it was in my homeland.

Adding a sense of intellectual presence to my library were reference materials and curated information sources such as encyclopedias on science, nature, and health as well as a range of Arabic and French dictionaries. Browsing through my encyclopedias often led me to explore topics I was not necessarily seeking. I credit my reading habits for helping me strengthen my vocabulary, language skills, and foundational knowledge—all valuable for common literacy, critical thinking, and communication.

My library at my parents' home in Jbeil, where it has remained to this day.

Besides reading, I also had more active hobbies. One of those was swimming. Every summer day, I would spend hours at the beach right below my house, with my brothers and our friends, appreciating the serenity of the water and contemplating the unknowns over the horizon, on the other side of the Mediterranean. Skiing provided a seasonal escape for me in the winter. I relished the quiet beauty of snowy mountain landscapes.

Regardless of the season, walking was a daily activity for me, a calming way to work through my thoughts. The mile-long radius around the rampart of the Old City, a short walking distance from my neighborhood, was my evening retreat. I found my solace midway on my route, in the garden behind Saint John Marc Church, where my family attended Sunday and holiday mass. I would simply lose track of how many times I had done the old city round or how long I had been in the garden.

The garden behind Saint John Marc Church in
Jbeil was my favorite quiet retreat.

None of this is to say that I was an isolated person, but I was someone who appreciated quality over quantity in friendships, naturally gravitating toward a smaller group of friends. The sport that truly captivated me was Rally Paper, widely popular in Lebanon at the time. These competitions are intensive, day-long, and team-based scavenger hunts that combine mental agility with driving acumen, making it unique and exciting. It also spoke to a side of me that appreciated strategy, creative problem solving, and teamwork. I was not the driver, but I was deeply involved in the intellectual side of the competition. A group of us formed two teams that competed and collaborated side-by-side, including my brother Bassam, my friend and classmate, Sarkis Azour, and Jamil Barhouche, who taught Sarkis and me French literature in high school. We trusted Fadi Sfeir and Hassan Mouawad to take command of the road with their precise vehicle control and defensive driving skills.

Arriving at the final destination of the 1980 Lehfed Rally Paper competition. I am standing next to the front passenger seat next to the driver, Fadi Sfeir. My brother Bassam is behind me, next to Hassan Mouawad.

In order to win a Rally Paper competition it is important to answer all the questions correctly and arrive ahead of others at the final destination. However, the ability to satisfy unusual requests can put a team over the top. In one competition, our team was the only group that managed to find the Sherwal pants, common among male villagers of Lebanon in earlier generations, which I wore.

Our job was to solve cryptic clues that took us through a series of stations where we would be handed a closed envelope containing a clue for the next station and a set of questions to answer on the way. These questions came from a range of topics including mathematics, science, history, geography, and politics. Because timing was also a performance factor, our driver focused on navigating the road, often under pressure, moving from one station to the next, as we submitted our answers, picked up our next clue, and received a new set of questions. The teamwork, trust, and problem solving required made each tournament a unique experience. Over the years, my team became well known in the area for our success in Rally Paper, going on to win every tournament for many years in a row. While my brother and others in the group excelled in the quantitative areas, I made my mark in humanities and the social sciences. We were different yet working as one. My mother was right.

CHAPTER 2

West Toward a New Home

My journey to the United States began exactly four months after I made the decision to leave Lebanon—on January 14, 1983. Now, with over four decades of reflection behind me, the date represents oddities, contradictions, and tensions arising as one world vanished and another appeared. I was apprehensive about starting a new journey to the United States. I was disappointed in myself that I was leaving my country, my family, and the only environment I had ever known—a world that was now in disarray, with those I loved at risk. Yet I was hopeful that I could re-create my life and my future, with the immediate goal of completing my studies. My intention was to eventually return to Lebanon trained, skilled, and experienced to my own personal and professional benefit, but also to contribute toward helping my country regain stability and prosperity.

I returned for the family I loved. I did not return to the Lebanon I knew. I will clarify. I carried the return-home intention with me through my education and early career phases, holding onto an image of growing old in the land that shaped me. But as the war dragged on, the country I knew began to change gradually, altered by painful milestones of the conflict. Each visit home became more unsettling, as nearly everything I was familiar with—people, institutions, government, the environment—grew distant and even harder to recognize. The worst of it was the destructive impact of the Syrian occupation on Lebanon. Their influence remained strong beyond the 1990 official end of the war and the start of Lebanon's reconstruction effort, sending a signal of what was to come over the next fifteen years. In 1991, the Treaty of Brotherhood, Cooperation, and Coordination ratified between Lebanon and Syria formalized their dominance and eroded Lebanese sovereignty. Syrian troops and intelligence services heavily influenced politics, elections, security, and fiscal decisions.

During the same year, the government passed a sweeping amnesty law that pardoned most crimes committed during the war, preventing accountability and reconciliation. The assassination of president-elect Rene Mouawad in November 1989 and the subsequent killings of political and religious Lebanese figures, both Muslim and Christian, reinforced a culture of violence and intimidation. In particular, Christian leaders who objected to Syria's *de facto* power broker role in Lebanon were either sent to jail or exiled. Former warlords who supported Syria's hegemony over Lebanon transitioned directly into political leadership roles, further unbalancing sectarian power structures. Elections throughout the 1990s and early 2000s were held under oppressive Syrian interference, as their leaders tailored electoral laws to dictate candidate selection and outcomes, severely weakening public trust in democratic institutions. Human rights abuses became the norm, along with kidnappings, arbitrary arrests, suppression of dissent, and restriction on free media.

Reconstruction and new infrastructure projects led to massive public debt. Complaints related to corruption and all aspects of governmental authority, including construction development, which primarily benefited Beirut, facilitated misconduct and deepened economic distress. The fact that the Lebanese state did not fully assert its authority and allowed some armed groups to retain their weapons as a resistance force against Israel's occupation in south Lebanon created a dual power structure and undermined state authority.

In time, I found myself not only separated by geography but by the quiet realization that the home I longed for no longer existed in the way I remembered it.

~

The day I left home, the sky itself seemed to mourn. Gray clouds hung low and heavy, motionless, as if the heavens refused to let go, just like I did. My suitcases were already packed, but in truth, I had only half-prepared. Purposely, I did not pack all of what I needed to bring with me, perhaps to reassure myself that my absence would not be for long. Yet, as I picked up my luggage, I felt the weight—family, home, memory, and a life I was leaving behind in a war-torn land.

The taxi that would take me to Beirut Airport pulled up slowly, settling outside our building. This chapter was ending. My mother wept. She insisted on coming to the airport to say her goodbyes. There was no convincing her otherwise. My father, who had always been close to his five boys, spent the entire day hovering around me, helping me pack. He said little, but his silence spoke volumes, carrying the kind of emotion that words could never fully express.

Where I lived in Jbeil, with a heavenly view of the Mediterranean Sea,
right outside the walls of the old city by the Phoenician harbor.

The drive to Beirut was just under an hour, but in that short span of time, we re-lived decades wordlessly. My mother sat beside me, staring straight ahead, clutching her purse as if it held the past itself. I stole glances at her, hoping she would not see me wiping away my tears, just as she was hoping I would not see hers. We both failed.

My world was collapsing in slow motion. The air carried the familiar scent of salt from the beach just meters away from my home. Every turn the car made unveiled another memory. Familiar streets echoed with the laughter of childhood friends. I reflected on endless summer days swimming in those waters until I saw my mother's red flag—her signature silent signal from our balcony that would summon us out of the sea and back inside for lunch. We would rest under the shade of the eucalyptus tree on our street, taking breaks from the intense midday sun, only to return to the water until dinnertime. By nightfall, I would sit on the low stone wall by the roadside to the old harbor, with my neighbor and friend Doumit Kallab, to watch people drift and drive down toward the water for a glimpse of the sunset while we sat quietly, already part of it, as if that moment might last forever. Through the car's window, tilting my head slightly backward, I watched my beautiful city fade as I glanced at the high winter waves of the Mediterranean crashing on the shoreline to my right.

Entering Beirut, after what felt like endless stops at military checkpoints, was like arriving in a city I could no longer recognize. The streets were filled with rubble, where once there had been streets filled with life and light. The beautiful downtown Beirut buildings that had once stood tall and proud were now reduced to ruins. The city I knew so well—from frequent visits with my paternal grandparents—was unrecognizable, scarred by a relentless civil war, torn further by a brutal occupation since June of 1976 by our neighbor to the north and east, Syria.

I thought of the last time I had been in this part of our divided capital city, now referred to as West Beirut. It was Christmas 1974, and I was celebrating with family at my grandparents' home in the Zkak el-Blat neighborhood, a mere four months prior to the start of the war. I was thirteen years old at that time. We had done such holiday gatherings there for as long as I could remember. My small family always celebrated all the major religious holidays with our larger family at my paternal grandparents' home, especially Christmas, Easter, and the Feast of Saints Peter and Paul—the namesakes of my father and uncle. The gatherings were always filled with apprehension and excitement. Apprehension because we had to be away from our own home and friends for these short periods, but excitement because, in addition to our grandparents and us, my uncles, aunts, and their kids came together to share the joy of these occasions. Spending time with our cousins, playing and talking, was always a highlight. We followed the usual holiday traditions of attending mass at Our Lady of Annunciation Greek Catholic Church, where I was baptized, visiting family and friends who lived in that part of the city, and enjoying the special holiday meals and desserts that my grandmother, aunts, and mother would create. Another highlight was the trip to nearby downtown Beirut, where we would marvel at the impressive holiday decorations displayed at churches and stores and along the streets.

I had not been to this neighborhood since. The war had divided nearly everyone and everything in our nation.

Outside my paternal grandparents' home in Beirut on Hosanna Sunday 1961. Only 37 days old, I am with my parents and older brother, Wadih (born in 1959).

In front of my paternal grandparents' home in Beirut on Hosanna Sunday 1963. I am on the left, entrusted with the family's traditional candle typical of the occasion, with my older brother Wadih, younger brother Bassam (born in 1962), and our father.

The Deek family grew again with the arrival of our brother Sami (born in 1964). I am in the front row between my older and younger brothers.

Christmas 1974 at my paternal grandparents' home in Beirut, our last visit there before the war broke out in 1975. I am in the back row, with my father and mother. In front of us, left to right, are my brothers Bassam, Sami, Roland (born in 1968), and Wadih. As on every special occasion, the cigar is evident between my father's fingers.

~

As we inched closer to the airport, my emotions were heightened as I saw the widespread devastation, both from the Civil War as well as from an invasion by Israel that was launched in June 1982, about six months earlier. By the time we reached the airport, the silence in the taxi had itself become language. At the terminal, my mother pulled me into a tight embrace. She said nothing. She did not need to. Her embrace said everything: that she loved me, that she feared for me, that a part of her would always be with me, even across oceans.

When I boarded the plane, it felt like I was walking into another life, one I had not yet imagined and was not sure I would even like. I was headed for the east coast of a distant continent, uncertain of what awaited me there. But I was hopeful. I knew I was moving toward peace, toward opportunity, toward something better, but I could not let go of the images racing through my head and the emotions running through my heart. The contrast between the home I knew and the one I was heading toward seemed irreconcilable. My heart grieved.

I tried to hold on to the beauty, the richness of life that had thrived in Lebanon before war tried to erase it. It was nothing short of extraordinary, a place where life pulsed through the streets like music. We lived on the coastal plains in the ancient city of Byblos in the shadow of the Mount Lebanon hills, snow-covered in winter, where the *Cedrus libani*, or the Cedars of Lebanon, once covered the entire landscape, green even in winter. In spring, the air was perfumed with citrus blossoms; in summer, jasmine vines bloomed and curled along street sides and balconies. The markets were always alive with people and chatter. Our Sundays were overtaken by church services, family lunches, loud conversations, and stories passed down like heirlooms. My childhood was filled with holiday gatherings that stretched from noon to midnight, children running amok while the grownups enjoyed homemade feasts, drank Arak, smoked cigarettes, and sipped coffee as they argued endlessly over politics and religion.

There was a sense of pride that lived within us, a love for our country and for each other. We believed in possibilities. Our cities were cultural mosaics, where neighbors honored each other's traditions. The tolling of church bells blended in harmony with the mosque's call to prayer. Education mattered. Art mattered. But above all, family mattered. Lebanon was a beautiful place, warm and prosperous. Then war snuck in like a thief in the night. It pitted neighbor against neighbor. It turned streets into front lines. Foreign boots trampled our soil with no regard for the people who called it home. It was not just bullets and bombs—it was betrayal, abandonment, and despair. The beautiful homeland created with blood and sweat by earlier generations was razed by internal greed and external envy.

All was in ruins.

~

Arriving at John F. Kennedy International Airport in New York City felt surreal. After hours in the sky, a sleepless night in Copenhagen, Denmark, on the way to catch the connecting flight, and then more hours in the sky, I landed in a world that seemed strangely orderly. The airport was bright, secure, and efficient. Everyone moved with purpose, faces expressionless, no one lingering. I was disoriented, exhausted. I carried a storm inside me that no one could see.

There was no cinematic moment of arrival, no triumphant "Here I am. I made it." Instead, there was paperwork and a frightening encounter. Being taken to a side room at JFK airport for an interview with an immigration officer was not on my itinerary, at least not the one I planned. There was a secondary inspection of my luggage and questions about the purpose of my travel, duration of my stay, financial situation, and where I would be staying. Though I managed to greet the inspector politely, but nervously, language barriers made it difficult to explain much beyond that. After some time, and with the help of a translator, it was finally determined that I would be welcomed to the United States of America.

After a quiet car ride with my brother Bassam to the apartment I would be sharing with him, the largest pizza pie I had ever seen was waiting on the kitchen table, alongside two of our cousins, Jamil and Jihad Hermes. They too had left Lebanon in the earlier days of the war to study in the United States.

But I had more important and timely things to do than eat pizza. I opened my luggage and pulled out the New Jersey Institute of

Technology Academic Catalog—now filled with underlined text, colored highlights, and my handwritten notes—sent to me while I was still in Lebanon by my brother who was already a student at NJIT. Immediately, I started to ask questions of everyone who was there about the courses I would soon be taking to complete my undergraduate degree and how long this might take. I admit that I must have looked, and sounded, like a geek, talking about academic plans, class schedules, and graduation dates before even taking a bite of dinner. But that did not matter to me. I was ready to start college, finish quickly, and return home as soon as possible. Every minute counted.

As if I were in a race with time, the next day I immediately turned my attention to improving my English reading and writing abilities, recognizing that these skills would be crucial for my success in college and beyond. Determined to make swift progress, I enrolled in an English as a Second Language (ESL) program at a small private school in Newark, located four city blocks away from NJIT, on the corner of Broad Street and Central Avenue. I attended classes five mornings a week for three months. Most of my classmates were immigrants with only a small number of them being there to prepare for college. Thus, the pedagogical style relied primarily on a conversational technique. In addition, I took a proactive approach to supplement my formal learning on my own with a focus on grammar, which I was able to do in the afternoons using self-guided resources at the NJIT Library. I dedicated myself fully to the process, steadily acquiring my new language skills.

Because my brother Bassam was already in the United States studying to be a civil engineer at the very school where I would earn my three degrees and later become a distinguished professor, dean, and provost, I had a connection to America that made my transition easier. At age nineteen, he had left Lebanon a year-and-a-half before I did, under similar circumstances. Two more brothers,

Sami and Roland, would soon follow our path in search of higher education opportunities in Montreal, Canada.

I prioritized my life to complete my studies, a goal I set for myself but just as urgently because I did not want to disappoint my parents. In Lebanon, education was not just a priority; it was our defining purpose. My brothers and I had been trained and conditioned from our earliest years to focus on school; everything else came second. Success was associated with enrollment at good schools. In our case, those administered by the Marist Brothers and other private institutions were our first and only choices. My parents sacrificed enormously to afford the tuition there, and so it should therefore be no surprise that they sold property and used whatever funds they could access to send four of their five children to study abroad during a very difficult period of instability and financial turmoil in Lebanon.

Let me be specific. When I arrived in the United States in 1983, my father had given my brother and me enough funds to cover one year of study—two semesters. Drawn on an account in Lebanon, the exchange rate was about L£4.50 to $1.00. Despite the war, the Lebanese currency was still relatively strong, although not as robust as the period before the war when it hovered at an average of a little over half that rate. Then the currency began to weaken, and quickly. By the summer of 1985, when I earned my BS degree, the exchange rate was L£20.00 to $1.00; L£250 in 1987 a year after I earned my MS degree; L£750 in 1990; L£1,800 in 1993; and then back down to L£1,500 soon after. It stabilized at that level and stayed there until August 2019. Still, this dwindling rate of exchange made it very difficult for parents in Lebanon to send money to their children studying abroad. The funds that my parents had set aside for our remaining semesters and my younger siblings' education became nearly worthless, retaining only a fraction of their original value.

By mid-1984, the inflation rate was running over 75 percent per year, and it got worse before it got better. By 1986, the economic consequences of the war in Lebanon caused a sharp decline in the GDP at a rate of -4.5 percent per year with an attendant inflation rate of nearly 20 percent per year. Unfortunately, the economic deterioration in Lebanon has continued into the present time, reaching a frightening and devastating peak in 2023, when the currency lost 98 percent of its value in a short period of time, between January 2023 and March 2024. This total collapse of the country's financial systems and institutions, including Lebanon's Central Bank, resulted in an exchange rate of over L£100,000 to $1.00 in 2023, retreating back to L£90,000 to $1.00 in 2025.

Fortunately for me, I had arrived in the United States years before this dire economic crisis spun out of control, which shielded my family from some of the financial burden. While still an undergraduate student, I secured two campus jobs—one in the university's bookstore and another in one of the research laboratories in the Department of Computer and Information Science, the Computerized Conferencing and Communication Center. This research center focused on how people interact through computers instead of face-to-face. It played an important role in the early development of what we now think of as online communication and virtual collaboration through its Electronic Exchange Information System (EIES). Later, as a graduate student, I became a teaching assistant, a post that carried tuition remission and a financial stipend. I became independent very quickly.

Yet even then, philosophically, I began to reflect more on the broader issues affecting Lebanon. I understood that my personal success could not be disconnected from the systematic failures that had made it incredibly difficult for others to follow a similar path. Even worse, the hyperinflation, plummeting currency, and declining purchasing power pushed so many of Lebanon's citizens into unexpected poverty. This also caused another wave of emigration.

In the background of my academic and personal journey were the socioeconomic and political inequities that, among other factors, propelled Lebanon towards a civil war. Though I understood the benefits associated with free market capitalism, I thought of all this as I ate the cold pizza on my first night in the United States; I was a believer in such an economic system. But I wondered then, and wonder now, about a system that neglects the individual as markets work their unseen forces.

Even then, I was wary of what unrestrained markets could do to individuals, and what could occur if governments did not accept their duties towards their citizens. My Lebanese upbringing and culture made me deeply aware that collectivism, not individualism, was most important to promote prosperity and stability in a society composed of communities with distinct, yet shared, visions for the future.

At that time, though early in my college career with limited means, experience, and expertise, I thought my focus had to be on completing my education and securing meaningful employment so that one day I could provide for my family's needs and be the best example I could be for my children and theirs.

CHAPTER 3

A Lebanese Student Abroad

The multifaceted nature of my Lebanese culture is reflected in the place where I arrived, and remained: New Jersey Institute of Technology. Among the nation's most diverse campuses, NJIT students differ in all imaginable ways, from race to religious belief, from income to cultural diversity. Baseball caps and hijabs are found in any classroom as students come together on a fifty-acre, tightly knit campus to do one thing well: prepare for productive careers in science and technology that will, in turn, amplify the potential for lifelong personal and professional growth. NJIT was unlike anything I had experienced before, yet I was there for the same purpose as the other students. That a large percentage of the student body was international, and that there was even a small cohort of Lebanese students, including some from my home city, offered a sense of comfort—a reassurance that I was not entirely alone. We were there to focus. We were there to work. We were there to succeed. Far from home, I was among my own.

There was, and still is, a firm belief on the NJIT campus in Newark, New Jersey, that research-based advances in science, technology, computing, and engineering hold the potential to improve the quality of life for everyone, and I wanted to be a beneficiary of this. At NJIT, I found the stability and community I needed to flourish, a place that sustained me through my BS and

MS in Computer Science, and PhD in Computer and Information Science, earned in 1997. It is also where I made my academic and administrative career over more than four decades.

~

When I joined NJIT in the early 1980s, it had already evolved significantly from its two predecessor institutions: initially Newark Technical School (NTS) and subsequently Newark College of Engineering (NCE). Naturally, NCE aimed to educate engineering students for noticeably different professions from NTS, whose craftsmen held titles consistent with its trade and vocational nature. Master's programs had gradually been introduced starting in the 1940s, followed by the launch of doctoral programs in the 1960s.

Because I have spent my life in the United States at NJIT, the history of this polytechnic institute is important to my story. In 1975, as Lebanon became a battleground, Newark College of Engineering, 5,700 miles away, became New Jersey Institute of Technology, reflecting the addition of the New Jersey School of Architecture and recognizing the emergence of new fields of study at NJIT, outside of engineering. Growing rapidly at its High Street location, NJIT remained overwhelmingly a school of engineering, despite the emerging disciplinary diversity, with a student and faculty population predominantly male and white.

In 1982, the year I decided to leave Lebanon, a third academic pillar, the College of Science and Liberal Arts, was founded to house the collection of NJIT disciplines that did not fit in engineering and architecture. A symbolic, but important, change followed in 1983, the year I arrived in the United States, with the city renaming High Street as Doctor Martin Luther King, Jr. Boulevard in honor of the late civil rights leader. NJIT had already been going through an evolution, and now just completed yet another transition from a college to a university.

By then, NJIT had a President, Dr. Saul Fenster, who was guiding the university with a clear vision, transitioning it from its teaching-focused roots to a new vision that included a meaningful research agenda. President Fenster, appointed in 1978, was held in high regard on and off the campus, and I was fortunate to work with him when I became a faculty member and administrator. He retired shortly before I became Dean of the College of Liberal Arts and Sciences in 2003. The impact of his steady leadership on our university, as well as on the city of Newark and the state of New Jersey, during the more than two decades of his presidency, is still often reflected on by many on our campus.

My first day on the NJIT campus was filled with a sense of gratitude. But it was also an introduction to a new world, in a number of ways. I was already thinking about how to better time my return trip from Newark to North Bergen, where I was living, so that I did not have another two-hour trip, that would make it a total of four hours round trip, using three different transportation modes—subway, train, and then a bus. First though, and more importantly, I needed to focus on getting through the day, buying my books, going to my classes, finding the library, and anything else that would come up. As I walked around, I noted the diversity of the people I was encountering. It had never seen people of so many different cultures and ethnicities in one place. And it was disorienting in other ways as well as I noticed the fast pace of my new world. As I continued to walk through the campus, I was observing how quickly people moved, in all directions, immersed in their own busy routines. I could not help but feel that everyone else had already found their place while I was still figuring things out.

Over the next few weeks, I became preoccupied with something else—settling on a major for myself. I knew that NJIT was primarily an engineering school, and I could not help but notice the slide rules of aspiring engineers were still visible in some shirt pockets on campus, both of faculty and students. These engineers would soon join earlier cohorts of NJIT graduates, skilled professionals dominating every aspect of the engineering landscape in New Jersey, with a respectable presence throughout the country. At the same time, scientific calculators had been appearing on the shelves of the NJIT bookstore, signaling a shift in tools and techniques.

It was evident that the pride in America's technological innovations and accomplishments during the 1960s and 1970s was responsible for the increased interest on the part of college-bound students in NCE's engineering disciplines. There was equally strong evidence that the disciplines fueling these accomplishments and driving innovations in the new digital world—computing, mathematics, and the sciences—were on the rise. It felt as if a transformation of a different kind seemed to be approaching, perhaps unbeknownst to many within and outside of the university. That shift captured my attention and my imagination. And so, I declared myself an aspiring computer scientist and began working to make that vision a reality.

My work in the Computerized Conferencing and Communications Center was another motivator. As an undergraduate student, my initial responsibility was to respond to external inquiries from individuals seeking information about the center's research and the researchers conducting it, Dr. Murray Turoff and Dr. Starr Roxanne Hiltz. One specific task I regularly carried out was mailing the CVs of these researchers. I was often struck by the sheer length and depth of those CVs. It was clear that I was working among highly accomplished computer scientists. This realization became a strong source of motivation for me to work harder and excel in my studies. It also reinforced my confidence that I had chosen the right major, as the research being conducted in the center aligned closely with my academic interests. Subsequently, I was able to join the development team that was designing the user interface for a new version of EIES. This allowed me to form many strong relationships with other students working there, a number of whom were my classmates. I also developed a close friendship with Anita Rubino, the business manager who hired me, and with whom I remained connected.

~

The opportunity to conclude my undergraduate degree in the United States was both exciting and frightening. Having been nudged in the direction of science, I had started my college education in Lebanon studying electronics technology but was interrupted because of the intensifying war. I knew that much of my coursework was relevant and could be transferred into my new curriculum, but I was unsure of exactly how much. For the first time in my life, I felt vulnerable. It was a difficult transition. I could manage the fundamentals in science and mathematics, but my new major, computer science, required that I handle devices that I had never seen before. The principal challenge, however, was the language. English was largely new to me.

When I left Byblos, I was midway through my college degree, with little to no English speaking or writing ability. French had been the main language of instruction at all my prior schools. Once I was on the NJIT campus, I found ways to improve my conversational English. I would put my watch in my pocket and sit in the campus center. When someone walked by, I would say, "Excuse me, do you know what time it is?" That was the opening for a brief conversation. Then I moved to another seat and waited for the next unwitting conversational English instructor. After asking everyone on the first floor, I graduated to the second floor. I did this repeatedly, slowly gaining confidence in my English skills.

This made me more comfortable to meet and speak with other people on campus, realizing that there were ample opportunities for me to practice my English skills and to share my knowledge. I soon learned about the lack of geographic, cultural, and historical awareness many people had beyond their American borders.

Their assumptions about life outside the United States were often surprising and sometimes amusing. I was shocked by how much of the world seemed unknown to my classmates.

A most interesting conversation happened when we were studying in one of the group rooms in our university library. My school friends wanted to know about my life in Lebanon. "Do you have ice cream in your country?" I was asked, with a puzzled look, as though the heat would make such a treat impossible, as though we did not have electricity or refrigeration. As baffling as it was, I took the opportunity to proudly share the beauty, advancement, and liberal nature of my Lebanese society, offering a new perspective on life in that part of the world. I spoke about the diverse landscapes, temperate climate, beaches, swimming in the summer and skiing on snow-capped mountains in the winter. Skiing seemed to flabbergast them the most. The idea of snow in Lebanon was so surprising to them that it left them speechless. Their mental map was that everything east of Europe was flat sand and oppressively hot, a land of dates and figs.

Another surreal conversation occurred around the topic of transportation. Some students genuinely wondered whether I traveled to school on a camel. They were stunned when I told them I had never seen a camel in my country, and that the first time I had seen one was in New York's Bronx Zoo. Watching their reaction, it seemed as if the very fabric of their reality had been challenged.

Each conversation became an opportunity to share the nuances of a place that was much more than the stereotypes they had in their heads. I did not mind explaining; I appreciated the chance to use these moments to educate, not just them, but also me as I saw these conversations as opportunities to improve my own language skills.

Also during this time, I got a job in the university bookstore. One day, a student came in and asked to buy a protractor. Not knowing what that word meant, I took the easy way out and said, "I am sorry, we are out of them." He pointed to the shelves above me and said, "You got hundreds of them; all you have to do is look." Feeling flustered, I said, "I apologize. They must have just arrived." But I actually was embarrassed for not understanding what the student was asking for, and even more so for not admitting it.

I must admit that this incident was a lesson that left a lasting impact on me. It got me thinking about the importance of clearly understanding each other, in both personal and professional settings. It transformed me into a more attentive listener, teaching me the value of truly understanding others rather than simply rushing to speak. This experience also taught me that I should not be embarrassed to admit that I do not know something. Even now, I find myself asking people to repeat and explain to me something they say which I do not understand, or even asking for the meaning and the proper use of a word or phrase that is new to me.

~

As my conversational English improved, I realized that there was a significant difference between that and scientific English. When attending classes, I understood very little of the content but faced the challenge head on by immersing myself in my schooling, in every possible way, to learn as much as possible and as quickly as possible. One of the courses I was placed into was English as a Second Language. "Encore," the instructor, Jim Wise, a playwright who I later learned was the composer of the musical *Dames at Sea*, would say at the end of my oral presentations. I was enthralled. I was consumed. When enrolled for credit in one section of a course, I asked the instructor to attend his or her other section as an auditor. I would hear it once, then a second time—and then, if there was a third section offered by another instructor, I audited that one, too. If enrolled for eighteen credits, it seemed I was actually taking three times that number. Often, I did not leave campus until 11:00 pm. As a transfer student, I spent four semesters and two summers completing my undergraduate degree. It was not until the end of that period—my graduation in the summer of 1985 with a BS in Computer Science—that I felt comfortable and confident in my use of English. With the credits that transferred from my prior college studies in Lebanon, I remained proud that I successfully completed my bachelor's degree in two years. I had found a new home and renewed hope.

Maura was by my side at my graduation with a Bachelor
of Science degree in Computer Science in 1985.

The pace and grueling nature of completing my degree were not new to me. In Lebanon, school was not just an institution of learning, it was a battleground. From an early age, Lebanese children learn that education is a means of securing the future, and as such, it is about surviving in a fiercely competitive environment. One of the defining characteristics of schooling in Lebanon was the intensity of the national examinations we needed to pass at different intervals of the grade levels. There were multiple major national exams between first grade and high school, each one marking a significant juncture in our academic life. What made these exams even more daunting was the fact that they were conducted on the same day throughout the entire country. This countrywide synchronization created an atmosphere that felt almost military in its precision. The exam papers were not just handed out at the usual school bell; they were delivered to each exam center by education ministry officials under strict protection by the police. As the time for the exams approached, the entire country seemed to hold its breath. For weeks, even months, before each exam, students and their families became consumed with preparation for these important life milestones.

The exams themselves were high-stakes, determining which academic path one would eventually follow in high school: a quantitative path that culminates in a "terminal" year in mathematics or experimental science or a literary path that culminates in a "terminal" year in philosophy and social science. The pressure to perform was communal; to prevail was to fulfill the hopes of the student, the family, and the community. Success meant respect, opportunity, and honor; failure left a lasting stigma. The atmosphere on exam days was surreal: high security, sealed exam papers, sharp attention to detail, and utter silence in the rooms as the exams began. Looking back, the intensity of those national exams taught me discipline, focus, perseverance, and how to handle pressure. But as I would learn later, there were other ways to examine, and be examined, that would not evoke such anxiety.

PART TWO

The Journey

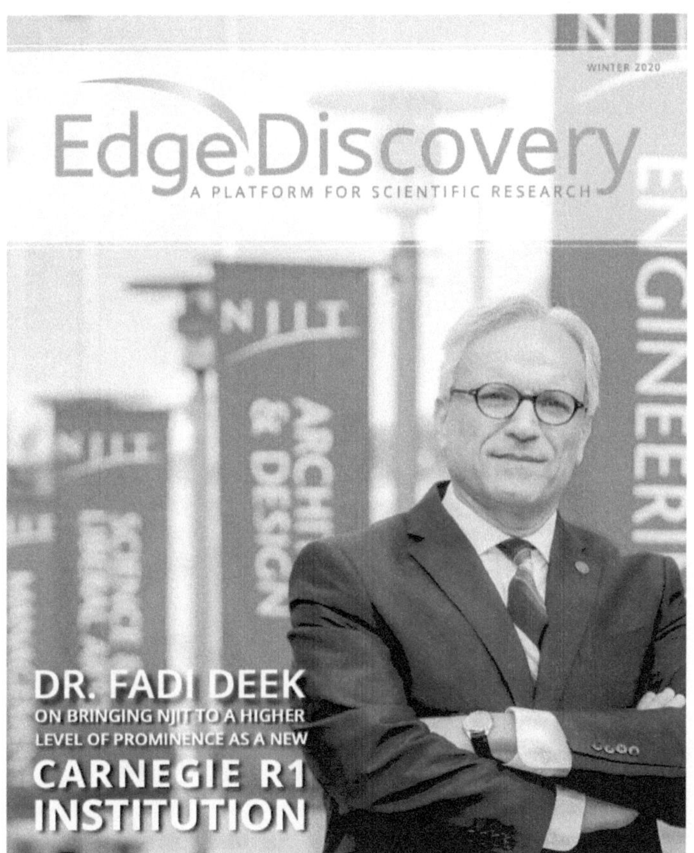

I have been privileged to be part of NJIT's remarkable progress over four decades. The higher education community took notice of this as a result of our *2020 Vision* Strategic Plan.

CHAPTER 4

The Other Side of the Desk

By January of 1985, less than a month after I earned my under-graduate degree, I was already teaching. Switching sides in the classroom, back and forth, from learning to lecturing, took some time to get used to. Like most people in higher education teaching, I received no formal training for the job. I was given my assignment as a teaching assistant very close to the start of the semester, a reflection on the junior nature of the position within the academic structure. With my first classroom assignment, I was given a textbook, two pieces of chalk, a room number, and a teaching schedule that began the next morning. I spent that day and a good part of the evening in the library reading books and making notes. Cutting short my preparation, the next morning came faster than I expected.

I do not remember many of the details about the earlier part of the day other than standing for what appeared to be a very long time in front of a classroom packed with students and running out of notes before the class session was over. Since then, on the first day of every semester I have taught, I have thought about that first day as the formal launch of my academic career. At the end of the course, I was pleased that students had not complained about my teaching and sometimes even offered their praise. Indeed, it was not until I became a graduate student and began working as a teaching assistant that I felt I had developed mastery of the spoken and written word in English.

Early into my career I was entrusted with teaching the fundamentals of computing courses required of all NJIT students.

As time passed, I learned the rhythm of my new country. I learned how to navigate new systems, speak a new language that was not inherently mine, smile when I did not understand, and ask for help when pride told me not to. Gradually, I began to feel a deeper sense of belonging. All this came with its own satisfaction and discomfort. I was going through a complex mix of emotions and caught between two lives, grateful and sorrowful. On one hand, there was the achievement resulting from my dedication to my educational pursuits, including earning multiple degrees and securing a job. On the other hand, there was this deep sense of sadness and realization that I would not be able to reconnect with my family and the familiar things I loved about Lebanon. Even though my success was something to celebrate, feeling torn between being proud of what I had been able to accomplish and grieving for what I was leaving behind made it feel bittersweet. Despite these challenges, many wonderful things soon followed.

In 1986, immediately after completing my MS degree in Computer Science, the Chair of the Computer and Information Science Department, at that time, professor James McHugh, made me an offer that immediately captured my interest: a full-time teaching position as lecturer with a commitment on my part to pursue a PhD.

My relationship with Jim McHugh had begun soon after I enrolled as an undergraduate student and continued to develop through all phases of my education. In my final semester of undergraduate study, we both had a chance to get to know each other well. I chose him as my senior project advisor and got to work closely with him for a full semester. Toward the end of that semester and closer to my degree completion, during one of our weekly meetings, he suggested that I should consider pursuing my master's degree. Having confidence in Jim's advice, I immediately applied and was accepted.

I had a chance to work with him again on my master's project while my primary advisor was on sabbatical leave. Our relationship continued to develop during my time as lecturer, as we worked together on various departmental initiatives. I subsequently selected Jim as my PhD advisor. He was a great mentor for my dissertation research. Most importantly, though, he was an incredibly generous colleague and a trustworthy friend. Outside of our computing pursuits, we often ventured into discussions on the topics of philosophy and logic, history and geography, theology and religion, politics and policy, and much more. Together, we were prolific writers of books and articles, but we enjoyed talking most about our respective families. He showed me what life in the academy could and should be. Jim's passing in 2022 has left a void that is difficult to fill.

~

I was still completing my undergraduate degree at NJIT when I met Maura Ann McShane, an Irish-American girl who was taking computer science courses as a bridge into the graduate program, having shifted her focus from environmental science to computer science. Our relationship had become more committed by the time I completed my master's degree.

When Maura and I began serious conversations about our future together, including getting married, I asked her if she would be willing to make a trip to Lebanon to visit my family, meet my siblings, and see where I was born and raised. The idea behind this was not just for her to understand my background but also to give her a chance to experience my country and culture firsthand, especially as we considered the possibility that we might, one day, return to live there. At the time, Lebanon was in the midst of a period of intense fighting, and its only international airport was unsafe for some people to travel through—specifically Christians—based strictly on their religious affiliation. So instead, our route would be to travel via the island country of Cyprus, about 150 nautical miles away from Lebanon, and take an overnight ferry to a city near where I lived.

I arrived a week ahead of Maura to ensure my family was ready to welcome her and to make her stay as comfortable as possible. As planned, Maura followed a week later. She was the only American on that ferry, traveling to a country where some parts were unsafe for Americans due to kidnappings, though not in the region where I grew up.

The journey itself was a true test of patience and perseverance for both Maura and me, but much more for her. On the day she was supposed to arrive, the sea was rough and the wind was strong, and the ferry made several failed attempts to dock at the small marina in Jounieh, about twelve miles north of Jbeil. The ferry then turned around and headed toward the larger and better equipped Beirut Port, another twelve miles to the north, only to be turned away because of fighting nearby that would prevent the passengers from disembarking. The ferry then returned to the original marina and, after numerous tries, finally managed to dock. Meanwhile, I was on the highway, parallel to the sea, driving back and forth mimicking the ferry's direction, not knowing what was happening until I was finally able to pick her up.

Despite the raging war in a number of areas in the country, Maura's two-week stay was filled with the warmth of family and the joy of the Christmas season. However, when it was time for us to leave, we faced another crisis. The small marina where we planned to board the ferry back to Cyprus and the surrounding city of Jounieh, were being heavily shelled on the day of our departure, preventing us from approaching the docks and boarding the ferry. We were kept on the lower floors of an adjacent concrete building for safety while security personnel arranged for us to be taken to the same Beirut Port the ferry had tried to dock at on its way in when the sea was rough. The journey to that port was terrifying. Under shelling and sniper fire, we were taken by buses with their lights turned off to avoid being seen by the snipers as we traveled along the highway. The tension reached new heights when we finally made it to the port, boarded, and set sail with lights out, under sniper fire again. Despite all the chaos and, at times, dangers surrounding us, Maura came shining through every part of the trip. Her calmness in the face of such circumstances strengthened my confidence in our future together. The best of it though is that she told me on her first day there that she could see herself living in Lebanon if that was the decision we ended up making.

Maura and I got engaged on our first trip to Lebanon in December of 1986. We were married in New Jersey on May 7, 1988, in the presence of our families and friends. We honeymooned in Ireland. Three miracles followed: Matthew Pierre, born on June

27, 1990; Andrew John, born on April 28, 1992; and Rebecca Ann, born on June 7, 1995.

Our wedding took place on May 7, 1988, in the presence of family and friends, including my parents and two brothers, who traveled from Lebanon.

~

Despite the distance and responsibilities to my growing family, I remained committed to Lebanon by visiting regularly and by taking up Lebanon's cause in the United States through student organizations, church activities, diaspora events, and political advocacy. While a student, I regularly wrote letters to my parents. and we often spoke on the phone, even though the cost was prohibitive. With time, the frequency of our conversations increased, eventually becoming daily with advances in technology and communication means. I also visited my family on a regular basis, usually during the Christmas holiday. I continued this practice even more frequently after getting married and having children but switched our visiting schedule to the summers, giving our children more time to develop a bond with their extended family—grandparents, uncles, aunts, and cousins—and also so they could enjoy the beach, as my siblings and I did when we were young. These visits intensified when our children, at a young age, demanded that they see their grandparents in Lebanon more frequently, which translated into more yearly trips for me because they wanted to travel to Lebanon both as a family and one at a time with me. Over the years, I grew more attached to my family abroad and to Lebanon the longer I was living in the United States.

Another milestone in my journey occurred on June 16, 1992, when I became an American citizen. The beautiful ceremony took place early in the morning at the Peter Rodino Federal Building on Broad Street in Newark, not too far from NJIT. I was joined by Maura, who is a second-generation American. When we walked into the room where those who were about to become citizens, their families, and United States Citizenship and Immigration Services staff were assembled, we were surrounded by people from all walks of life—different races, colors, accents, physical traits, and attire. I was immediately transported back to my early days in the United States, with all the emotions I experienced then: excitement, apprehension, hope, and much more. What really stood out to me were the remarks made by the judge who was administering the Oath of Allegiance to the United States of America. I was surprised when he encouraged everyone there to hold on to their original citizenships in addition to the new one we had just earned, if this was allowed by our native nations. While I was somewhat surprised to hear this, it made me feel proud and relieved, since my home country, Lebanon, supported dual citizenship. Knowing that I could be an American without rejecting my Lebanese heritage put me at ease.

After the ceremony, Maura and I met up with Joan Matas, a close friend from NJIT, and her mother for lunch at a special restaurant by the water in Secaucus, New Jersey. My friend's mother, an attorney and a remarkable person, had helped me with my citizenship application, as she had similarly volunteered her time to help many others. Later in the afternoon, I returned to NJIT to teach my summer session class. For me, it felt like such a fitting way to conclude the celebration.

The period of my PhD studies began when Maura was pregnant with Matthew and extended past the birth of Rebecca. While it was a complex academic endeavor, it also was fulfilling as Maura and I worked and raised three young children. Looking back, I realize it was also a family affair that created a nurturing environment where knowledge was part of our daily lives, which played a critical role in our children's intellectual development.

One of the most cherished parts of our day was the customary family dinner and what came before and after. Preparing our meals was a family affair. My cooking skills, initially honed in my mother's kitchen and later perfected in my college days, came in handy. Maura showed her dexterous hands in the kitchen by baking the most delicious desserts, including the kids' birthday cakes. Using my creative skills, I was able to decorate their cakes in any way they wanted. Together, we turned simple ingredients into artistic pieces. The kids watched, helped, enjoyed, and learned. We created a space where learning was not a burden but something to be explored. After dinner, we would gather in a room right next to the kitchen and dive into our work, with classical music playing softly in the background.

As our children were growing up, we did our homework together. They worked on their math and science and wrote their essays. I studied for my doctoral qualifying exams and worked on my dissertation on software development and learning systems. Through it all, Maura was there for each of us, steadfast and supportive.

We had a large, lit world globe in the middle of the room. This scene became a gateway to meaningful conversations about other countries, languages, weather patterns, and geographical diversity. We would talk about people, political systems, religions, and different ways of life. These were always conversations, never lectures, that felt natural and sparked curiosity that expanded our understanding of the world around us but also about cultural differences and similarities. We talked until it was time for our children to move on to their bed-time routine and for me to move to my basement office. Needless to say, my homework went way past our children's bed time. Looking back, it is clear how much this time shaped our family and the life Maura and I built together, step by step.

In order to support my growing family while working as a full-time lecturer at NJIT, I also taught as an adjunct instructor at Rutgers, the State University of New Jersey, and Middlesex College. My typical teaching load was seven courses per semester, often even more—a testament to the work ethic I embraced, truly the hustle of an immigrant. My wife, a talented computer scientist herself, helped me study for my doctoral qualifying examinations by annotating my readings while I was working. Her notes helped me to focus my studying on the essence of the material and ensure my knowledge was current. I passed all eleven topics of the exam and moved on to the dissertation stage. I earned my PhD in 1997. I was thirty-six years old.

~

Following my doctoral completion, I was appointed to the faculty and given a new title of Vice Chair of NJIT's Department of Computer and Information Science. This was the largest and fastest growing academic unit of the university at the time. Because of my extensive administrative role in the department during the prior decade, in addition to teaching, the chair of the department and the dean of the college, who were both very supportive of my faculty appointment, did not want to lose my academic and administrative leadership contributions. No one in the department, or at the university, had held such a title until then. Thinking of it now, I am surprised that I was given such a role prior to earning tenure.

As a faculty member, I was placed on the second rank of the scale, associate professor, skipping the first rank of assistant professor, at the recommendation of Provost Gary Thomas. Putting even more tension in the system, as he would have put it, I was expected to earn tenure on an accelerated clock, within three years. My first attempt would be during my third year and, if I did not prevail then, a second and final attempt would be extended to me during my terminal year.

When I received and read those details in my appointment letter, I felt overwhelmed and uncertain about what lay ahead. Regarding time to tenure, I wondered whether I would have been better off starting at the assistant professor level, which would have afforded me twice as much time and three shots at tenure according to the norms of that era. I immediately wrote Provost Thomas asking for a clarification:

> Date: 01 Oct 1997 10:36 PM
> From: "Fadi P. Deek" <deek@admin.njit.edu>
> To: "Gary Thomas" <thomas@admin.njit.edu>
> Subject: Question
>
> Dr. Thomas,
>
> I received, signed, and returned to your office the letter regarding my tenure consideration. The letter mentions that I have 2 shots (and not 3) at tenure. Is this what you intended?
>
> Thank you,
> Fadi

The next day, as he did so often over the years, his response gave me the confidence I needed:

> Date: Oct 2, 1997, 2:04 PM
> From: "Gary Thomas" <thomas@admin.njit.edu>
> To: "Fadi P. Deek" <deek@admin.njit.edu>
> Subject: RE: Question
>
> Fadi:
>
> The letter follows the Handbook rules. I have confidence in you that 2 is 1 more than you need.
>
> Gary

I still had to wait three years to know that he was right.

Gary Thomas was a respected figure on our campus—brilliant, accomplished, and humble. He was the first person to assume authority over the entire enterprise of academic affairs at NJIT, and the first to hold the title of provost. Saul Fenster entrusted Gary with crafting the strategy to steer NJIT into a research university. I very often think of Gary. There are things I see, things I do, or things others do that remind me of Gary's graciousness, modesty, and sense of humor. To me and many others, Gary was a beacon of wisdom and kindness whose lessons I reflect on to this day.

I think of Gary every time we have an NJIT commencement. I remember how as soon as the ceremonies concluded, I would see Gary, unworried about the celebrities on stage, almost run down to where department administrators and registrar's staff were already assembled, behind tables, distributing diplomas to graduates. I would watch Gary walk between the rows of tables, shaking hands with every person there, and thanking them for their work. Gary's graciousness was always evident. On his last day as provost at

NJIT, he walked the campus, building by building, floor by floor, going from one office to another, even returning to some offices twice to make sure he saw everyone, just to say goodbye and thank you.

I met Gary early in my career at NJIT, in 1988, at his request, while I was serving as Director of Undergraduate Programs in my department. Those were exciting times for computer science, which saw remarkable growth both academically and industrially. NJIT's enrollment in computing-related majors benefited tremendously from this growth. Gary was interested in the impact of these developments on our curriculum. I was at the time teaching the fundamentals of computer science sequence, and he asked me to come over and talk to him about it, and he did this frequently.

Gary supported me during and after my PhD work. Soon after my dissertation defense, which he attended, he invited me to an off-campus lunch where we talked about the future. Gary brought with him a series of books on electrical engineering that he had written and encouraged me to write about computer science. We talked about the process of writing, of scholarship and research. His guidance has greatly helped me in my career. I will remember Gary for his mentorship, not only with me but also with many other faculty members he helped develop professionally, in terms of teaching, scholarly activities, and external funding potential, as well as in terms of service and administrative leadership.

In 1998, Gary invited me to join him on a professional trip to the Philippines, where we were to meet with higher education officials and establish a relationship with a private technological university. All arrangements had been finalized well in advance. The timing was particularly tight because our departure was set for just one day after I returned from a trip to Montreal, Canada, where I had the honor of serving as godfather to my niece, Bernadette. On the day of my return, severe ice conditions at the Montreal Airport caused repeated and prolonged delays. What began as incremental postponements extended into a delay of more than a full day. As the hours passed, it became clear that the cascading delays would significantly compress the already narrow window between landing at home and departing again. By the time we were set to leave from Newark Airport, equally severe weather, frigid and icy, had arrived in the United States as well, both locally and nationwide, which caused considerable disruption to air travel, including our own. When I finally took off from Montreal, I realized I would not have enough time to go home, drop off my luggage from the first trip, and retrieve the luggage for the next one. In an effort to salvage the situation, I called Maura and asked her to drive to Newark Airport with my Philippines luggage and take my Montreal luggage back home. Despite the coordinated exchange at the airport, which included some quick hugs and kisses to Maura and the kids who had joined her on the drive up to Newark, I still missed my scheduled flight. Gary had departed, delayed but still as planned. I quickly purchased a new ticket and found my way to the next available flight.

Despite the weather concerns, we both arrived and reconnected at our destination in Manila, but without our luggage. I was lucky; the next day at least one of my bags was delivered. But not Gary's. I had two suits with me and I offered one to Gary, which he wore. I remember the pants; even with the cuffs let out they only reached above his ankles. But although I had brought two suits, I had only brought one pair of dress shoes, which I was not about to share with Gary. You can imagine the sight with both of us going around from one meeting to another—Gary in my suit jacket and ankle-length pants, worn with his white sneakers, long before it became the fashion. I remember the looks people gave us. But Gary met it all with his usual warmth and a smile.

We had gone to the Philippines via Newark/Hong Kong/Manila but we returned through Manila/Beirut/Newark, and made a planned stop in Lebanon. We visited universities and met with the President of Lebanon, Elias Hrawi. Gary was as presidential as the president of the country, discussing regional issues with sophisticated insight and remarkable grace, as Kipling described in his poem "If"—he was the kind of man who could "walk with kings—nor lose the common touch." He passed on New Year's Day, 2008. I will miss him forever.

On our 1998 visit to Lebanon, Provost Gary Thomas and I met with Lebanese President Elias Hrawi to discuss the role of science and technology in Lebanon's post-war recovery.

During our visit in 1998, Gary Thomas admired the efforts of rebuilding downtown Beirut but was especially charmed by Raouché's Pigeon Rocks, the iconic natural landmark of two massive limestone formations in the Mediterranean Sea.

Two other people are similarly credited with impact on my career at NJIT. Urs Gauchat, Dean of the College of Architecture and Design and John Poate, Dean of the College of Science and Liberal Arts. Not that Gary Thomas needed any prodding, but I am aware that they both proposed to him, and endorsed his decision, to keep me on the university faculty subsequent to my PhD completion, which is a fairly uncommon thing to do.

Dean Gauchat joined NJIT in 1991, and I had the pleasure of meeting him shortly thereafter. At the time, I was teaching the first computer science course taken by all students in his college. He was remarkably engaged and took the initiative to learn directly from me about the course content. In return, he shared his thoughtful insights on what he believed his students needed in order to thrive in their chosen field.

I was deeply impressed by that initial conversation. Urs was knowledgeable, well-informed, and thoughtful, always approaching conversations with openness and mindfulness. While he often held strong opinions on this topic and many others, Urs was always respectful and genuinely open to alternative viewpoints. If presented with a well-reasoned argument, he did not hesitate to reconsider his position.

Over the years, I often found reasons to reach out to Urs, ostensibly to provide updates on the course his students were taking. In truth, my real motivation was to benefit from his insights. Urs was an eloquent conversationalist, always welcoming and intellectually generous. Our connection evolved when he served as interim dean of the College of Science and Liberal Arts (CSLA). That role gave us more opportunities to collaborate, and our professional relationship grew even stronger when I later became Dean myself, regularly turning to him for counsel. We remained close throughout his tenure and have continued to stay in touch following his retirement in 2016.

After several attempts, NJIT successfully recruited John Poate, in 1996, to lead our College of Science and Liberal Arts. Dean Poate, a distinguished scientist with expertise in nuclear physics, solid-state physics, and materials science, came to us from Bell Labs. He was exceptionally sharp, highly accomplished, and impressively well-versed in a wide array of scientific and technological disciplines.

I did not know John before he joined NJIT. However, his administrative assistant called to set up an appointment for me with him in his first week. At the time, I was serving as Assistant Chair and Director of Undergraduate Programs. I do not recall all that we discussed, but one thing he wanted to know was about my plan to conclude and defend my PhD dissertation. I found this question surprising, as well as how much he seemed to know about me and my work at NJIT. Of course, this became clearer knowing about his efforts, among others, to keep me at NJIT subsequent to my doctoral completion.

As this was his first academic appointment, John often reached out to me to discuss the cultural and organizational nuances of academia, particularly those unique to NJIT. Through these frequent conversations, we developed a close friendship. We spoke or met almost daily, often taking long walks together around campus and through Newark, engaging in conversations that spanned our diverse interests, from science and technology to history and the arts. The Newark Museum was a frequent destination, especially when new exhibits were on display.

Regrettably, John was eventually recruited away by a semiconductor manufacturing company and later assumed the role of Senior Vice President for Research at a competing polytechnic university. Despite his departure, we remained close. After I became Dean of CSLA, following in his footsteps, I invited John to serve on the college's advisory board. More significantly, John became a trusted and essential advisor to me during my tenure as Provost, offering invaluable guidance on matters of cutting-edge science and technology. To this day, we remain in regular contact.

~

Fueled by a commitment to teaching, success in research, a record of dedicated service, and evidence of leadership, I was rewarded with a sequence of increasingly consequential academic and administrative appointments. In 2000, I was appointed Chairperson of the Information Technology Program, and in 2001, Associate Dean of the newly created College of Computing. In 2003, I was promoted to full Professor and became Dean of the College of Science and Liberal Arts. A decade later, in 2013, I was appointed Provost and Senior Executive Vice President and received the pinnacle faculty rank of Distinguished Professor. By then, I had been working at NJIT for twenty-seven years.

Maura and I were a yearly fixture at Celebration, a major fund-raising event for scholarships at NJIT. Our family has endowed three scholarships—in our parents and our own names. This picture is from 2013, the year I became provost.

CHAPTER 5

Community and Colleagues

I have been privileged to serve in numerous roles at New Jersey Institute of Technology, from entry-level to executive, allowing me to gain a comprehensive understanding of university functions and organizational structure. In my academic role, I can say that I literally carried out every possible function in education and research, from the rank of lecturer to distinguished professor. Similarly, I performed every possible duty as an administrator from coordinator to provost and senior executive vice president.

While I have spent my entire professional career at NJIT, I have found our work culture, based on my interactions with colleagues at other academic institutions, to be unique. One aspect that left an impression on me is how seamless and welcoming it was for me to transition from a student to an employee. Specifically, how normal it felt to be working closely with people who had taught me only a few semesters earlier. Even as I moved up through the ranks, these very same people were not only supportive but proud. Rightfully so, they took credit for my success. I could not have been more indebted and honored.

My academic leadership capabilities were honed and tested over two decades at the highest levels of the university organization. The prior period, nearly as long, was instrumental in my development as a teacher, researcher, and college-level administrator.

~

I was lucky to move very quickly on the academic ladder in the College of Computing. I spent the first eleven years of my profession at the university in a series of teaching and administrative positions. In addition to lecturer, my first position to which I was appointed, I also held the titles of coordinator, director, and assistant chair in the Computer and Information Science Department, the predecessor to the current College of Computing. In 1997, having completed my PhD, I was offered a tenure track faculty position at the rank of associate professor, with a short time to tenure. An administrative assignment was immediately added to that faculty role: vice chair of the department, a newly created title to help manage the largest and fastest growing academic unit of the university.

Within three years of joining the faculty, I received tenure, in recognition of my education and research contributions. Immediately after, the Department of Computer and Information Science evolved into the College of Computing, with the institution acknowledging the overall transformation our computing discipline was undergoing but also noting its importance to our university in terms of research potential and growth in student enrollment. Upon appointment of the inaugural dean for our new college, I was asked to join him at the helm as associate dean, which I accepted.

Within three more years, I was promoted to full professor in recognition of my education, research, and leadership accomplishments. To my knowledge, this was the fastest tenure and promotion timetable at the university, at least in recent history. A decade after, my teaching, research, and leadership were recognized with a promotion to the rank of distinguished professor.

During the early days of my career, I found myself interacting and working directly with university leaders who held titles multiple levels above mine, giving me a comprehensive perspective that few others had. I believe this was a rare opportunity that allowed me to gain experience in positions of increasing responsibility. These many roles helped me develop a detailed understanding of how the university functioned. Additionally, working with and leading a large number of people, each with a range of abilities and personalities, provided me opportunities to grow. Observing how others managed and behaved, learning both the things that I should do and the things I should not, was a powerful way to improve my own leadership skills. This experience allowed me to integrate best practices of leadership into my own work style by consciously embodying the qualities and behaviors I wanted to practice but also cultivate in others.

~

A pivotal moment occurred in 2003, shortly after my promotion to full professor. Toward the end of the fall semester, I received a phone call from the university provost, William Van Buskirk, asking if I could come to his office for a meeting with him. I wondered about the nature of the conversation. Despite my role as associate dean, a provost interacts with the college deans regarding matters concerning their units.

When I got to his office, he shared with me that one of our university deans had just stepped down, and that he and President Saul Fenster were extending an offer for me to leave my College of Computing position and return to the College of Science and Liberal Arts to help put the college back on track until a permanent dean could be appointed. I say return to CSLA because this is the college that was home to my department before it became its own college, and more importantly, it was where I had spent my student years, earning my undergraduate, graduate, and doctoral degrees.

I was not anticipating this offer. Bill asked me to think about it over the weekend and return to him. I made it clear that I did not want to leave my dean stranded, and so suddenly as well.

To impress upon me the seriousness of this request, in a friendly manner, he shared a simple statement: "Neither I nor the president can accept no for an answer." My appointment had also been discussed at the most recent Board of Trustees meeting, I promptly was informed.

I held the utmost respect for Bill, a distinguished graduate of the United States Military Academy and a former active-duty officer in the United States Air Force. He had previously entrusted me with the leadership of the university's interdisciplinary Information Technology Program, and I was committed to meeting, and exceeding, his expectations. More importantly, I viewed this as a meaningful opportunity to work more closely with him and to contribute to his vision for the university. Thus, I accepted the position as offered. While William Van Buskirk signed my initial appointment letter as interim dean of CSLA, it was Urs Gauchat who signed my appointment letter as permanent dean, during his service as interim provost after Bill elected to conclude his distinguished academic career back on the faculty side.

In 2004, less than one semester after I assumed the role of dean in the College of Science and Liberal Arts, the provost position became vacant, and a search firm was retained to assist in finding a candidate to serve in that role. A short while after, the consultant leading the search was on campus to meet with relevant stakeholders, listen to their ideas regarding the position and the person they believed we should seek, and help our campus prepare to launch a national search to fill this important role. On his first day on campus, the search consultant called my office and requested a meeting with me, to take place right after his first meeting of the day, which was with President Robert Altenkirch, at NJIT's helm since 2002. The timing of the meeting and its order conveyed the implied message to come.

I was invited to become an applicant for the position. While I was truly flattered, I did not need any time to think about this: I politely declined to consider the opportunity, offering two reasons. First, my young family; and second, I had already committed to CSLA. I still recall his reply: "You are a wise man."

Throughout my career at NJIT, and up until this period, I viewed myself as a soldier of the university and accepted my next responsibility as assigned by university leadership. I was loyal but I had always put family first, unabashedly known to all who knew me both within and outside the university. In fact, given my past trajectory, and in anticipation of what more might come, Maura and I had discussed the future, and we both agreed that greater professional commitments or a higher-level position, at that time, might come at the expense of our children. Our decision was easy to make and thus we agreed that I would remain in my current position until our youngest child, Rebecca, finished high school. We were nowhere near that point. She was still in elementary school. Moreover, I had just arrived at CSLA and made a commitment that I would be there until that college had found its next leader, a process that usually took about a year. My intention was to return to my home, the College of Computing, after that. However, that timeline did not work out exactly as I had planned. I ended up staying at CSLA for a decade.

Upon arriving at CSLA, I was told many things by many people, but the one comment that made an impression on me was the observation that "the college is directionless and demoralized." The decision for me to leave the College of Computing was a difficult one, and the challenges in CSLA initially seemed formidable. Still, I was determined to engage in an immediate academic and administrative revitalization initiative to address the "directionless" concern. With the support of the faculty, staff, students, and alumni, I launched a faculty and staff strategic steering committee in which I actively participated. This committee developed the first comprehensive five-year strategic plan for the college. An important goal of this plan was to evolve the college beyond its original role as a primarily service unit that provided courses in mathematics, the sciences, and humanities to the broader university community.

Understanding that highly qualified, highly motivated students are attracted to programs that offer the best potential for career success, and having experienced similar success in the growth of computing programs, particularly the Information Technology Program, for which I served as founding Chair, we proposed a plan that would develop new programs and specializations, target curricular modifications, and foster the development of a strong culture of assessment to measure progress toward our goals. To that end, we added new career-viable degree programs consistent with the college's research strengths and the needs of the economy in the state, region, and nation.

With the academic portfolio expanded, I focused on other initiatives, including our new pre-service teacher preparation option with a focus on STEM (science, technology, engineering, and mathematics), consistent with NJIT's character, in collaboration with our colleagues in the Urban Education Department at Rutgers-Newark. Our expanded pre-professional options, such as pre-health and pre-law, created a unique environment in which students were prepared to pursue professional degrees through any undergraduate major offered in CSLA. Other initiatives were also launched to further the excellence in our graduate and doctoral programs and to enhance the quality and quantity of enrolled students.

The "demoralized" concern I had encountered was regarding the sudden and significant loss of enrollment in CSLA when the Department of Computer and Information Science, its largest member, evolved into its own independent College of Computing, my new academic home. This left CSLA with about three percent of the total university enrollment, with an additional cohort of students placed there in a holding pattern as undeclared majors until they were able to matriculate in their programs of choice, usually in engineering and computing. However, as strong academic programs emerged throughout the college, enrollment trends began to reverse. During the first cycle of strategic planning, the size of the entering first-year class quadrupled compared to the average size of the previous five years, more than tripling the overall enrollment.

The corollary objective to increasing enrollment was enhancing the academic profile of entering undergraduate students. This effort also saw tremendous success, with the enrollment rising one percentage point a year and stabilizing at a little over twelve percent of NJIT's total student population by the end of the second cycle of strategic planning. Even more encouraging was that the average SAT score of the entering class also increased to a height achieved by the university as a whole seven years later, going from the lowest average to the highest within a decade.

~

I attribute the successes we achieved in CSLA to the entire college community, which was eager to reconceive its role, direction, and priorities to move forward beyond a past that saw the college struggle with attracting and retaining strong leadership at its helm. In the decade prior to my appointment as dean, a total of eight people served as deans, three in a permanent capacity and five as interim. The situation was different in the academic departments making up the college, with historically excellent chairpersons and committed faculty leaders across the college. What CSLA needed was unity around a shared ethos, and the entire community was ready to do this. Throughout this period, I routinely sought the counsel of accomplished college administrators to test my ideas on and benefit from their experiences. Among them, Daljit Ahluwalia, a respected figure on our campus, stood out as a particularly generous and influential mentor.

I first met Daljit when we both were appointed to our very different positions at the university—he as professor and chair of the Department of Mathematical Sciences, and me as lecturer, while concurrently pursuing my PhD. Daljit was a distinguished scholar, recruited from the famed Courant Institute of Mathematical Sciences at New York University to help elevate and enhance the visibility and reputation of our own department. Although we were based in different academic units, he consistently took a genuine interest in my doctoral progress and professional development. He served as a true mentor to me, offering strategic guidance shaped by his own extensive professional experiences. Over the years, we occasionally collaborated on initiatives that advanced the goals of our respective departments, for example, the successful dual undergraduate degree in mathematics and computer science.

Daljit and I shared common ground as immigrants to the United States, bonded by mutual appreciation for the opportunities this country provided to our families. Sometime after my promotion to full professor, he graciously extended an invitation for me to hold a joint appointment in his department, an offer I was honored to accept. Soon thereafter, upon my appointment as dean of CSLA, home to his department, I had the privilege of working more closely with him on strengthening research and attracting promising new faculty to raise the college's academic profile. His thoughtful counsel proved invaluable in many key decisions I made both as dean and later as provost. Even after his retirement, Daljit and I remained close friends and continued to stay in regular contact. Daljit passed in 2025, leaving behind a distinguished personal and professional legacy.

I also harnessed the energy and wisdom of respected senior faculty in deliberating the college's strategic priorities, working with them to involve the CSLA community at large in these discussions. Denis Blackmore and Norbert Elliot, faculty leaders representing the two intellectual sides of the college, the sciences and the liberal arts, were instrumental in working closely and strategically with me, as we set out to bring about a transformation at the college.

I had known Denis, a highly respected professor and researcher in the Department of Mathematical Sciences, for more than two decades, essentially for as long as I had been at NJIT by that time. I met him when I was a student, got to know him better when I became a lecturer, but our relationship developed and strengthened during the decade in which I served as Dean of CSLA. With our offices located on the same floor, we spoke frequently, exchanging ideas and insights. Denis and I co-chaired the committee that developed the college's first strategic plan, an initiative that helped develop a clear and ambitious path forward for CSLA.

When you are a dean, it is natural for people to seek your support for their individual needs and priorities. Understandably so. However, when Denis came to me with a request, it was never on his own behalf. His concerns were always for others, typically an undergraduate student who was pursuing research with him to attend a conference; or a research collaborator from a different institution who wished to visit our campus; or a junior faculty member, a rising star, that he hoped to retain at NJIT. This selflessness and deep sense of community were hallmarks of Denis' character.

Our personal and professional relationship continued to evolve when I assumed the role of provost and senior executive vice president. Denis served as vice president and then president of the Faculty Senate during the COVID-19 pandemic. From the administration's point of view, we could not have had a better faculty leader to partner with in such an unprecedented moment. As he had always done before, Denis provided consistent and thoughtful leadership during this difficult time. Denis passed in 2022, a loss to our academic community.

In 2003, Norbert Elliot was a prolific researcher in CSLA's Department of Humanities and Social Sciences and a respected senior faculty member in his department. where he had served multiple terms as chair. I first met Norbert early in my career when we both served on one of the university's professional accreditation committees focused on undergraduate education. Our collaboration deepened when we jointly mentored a graduate student through her professional and technical communication master's thesis.

After I arrived at CSLA, Norbert quickly became a valued friend, research collaborator, and co-author working with me on shaping the strategic objectives of CSLA. Norbert and I shared a commitment to the role of assessment in supporting data-informed decision making. This mutual perspective proved vital in quantifying our strategic priorities and gauging our progress toward these goals. He and I co-chaired the committee that developed the college's ambitious second strategic plan.

Toward the end of my tenure as dean, we teamed up again to lead another cycle of the university's regional accreditation, serving as co-chairs of the steering committee, further strengthening our partnership. Our daily morning meetings, over tea, were very productive, as we discussed and worked on administrative and scholarly matters. Norbert and I were also able to maintain our research activities, and together we mentored a PhD student toward completing her dissertation.

This collaboration continued as I transitioned into the role of provost and invited Norbert to join me as a senior advisor to the provost. In this role, during the early stages of my appointment, Norbert and I had the pleasure and satisfaction to tackle together one major project with far-reaching university implications, the *2020 Vision* strategic plan. He took charge of crafting and disseminating for discussion the major threads of our plan and synthesizing community feedback, a role he fulfilled with great insight and dedication before his subsequent retirement. Norbert's departure from campus disrupted my daily routine. I missed our 7:30 am morning tea ritual, during which I served green tea in mugs on a tray that he and his wife had gifted me when I was his dean. Norbert always made any conversation special.

I made a most fulfilling leadership decision when I realized that my time in CSLA was going to be lengthier than I had anticipated. I had a concern about the future of the Information Technology program I was leading. The program was relatively new but performing exceedingly well. However, it still did not have any faculty affiliated with it, with one administrator assigned exclusively to the task of academic advising. I worried that my departure would hinder its growth. Instead of holding on to both the program and the college I was expected to lead, I recommended a close colleague, Rob Friedman, to take over. He was already working alongside me, running a multimillion-dollar grant funded by the State of New Jersey that involved university-wide initiatives in education and research.

Rob came from a different educational background and academic experience. With a PhD in literature, he was a lecturer in our Department of Humanities. I had just made the transition from lecturer to faculty, after completing my PhD, and Rob was instrumental in helping me think of my dissertation as both a cohesive document and a collection of autonomous pieces fit for publication. This relationship quickly developed into a productive collaboration, especially as we coalesced around the idea that what we teach, he composition and me computing, actually share commonalities that not many appreciate. This prodded Rob to invest effort in understanding the intricacies of his new environment. He even went on to earn a master's degree in Information Systems, and I served as his thesis advisor.

Rob's transition into Information Technology was seamless, and the program continued to thrive. What stood out was not just his ability to take on the responsibility, but the way he grew into the role. His hard work and dedication did not go unnoticed. When a faculty opening arose in the Department of Humanities, we both recognized it as an opportunity for Rob to return to CSLA. He quickly rose through faculty and administrative ranks, as his excellence became evident there too.

~

In 2009, we had another vacancy in the provost position with the departure of yet another officeholder. Soon after, nominations for different representatives of our university stakeholders were solicited by the Faculty Council to serve on the search committee. My name was among those forwarded to the president as a potential committee member representing the deans. However, I later learned from the Faculty Council president that when their leadership met with him, the president did not wish me to serve on this committee as he had hoped to see me as a candidate this time around. By then, I was well established at CSLA, enjoying very much what I was doing, the results of our collective efforts, and the strong support of the college community. I opted to serve on the search committee.

In fact, I had just initiated our second five-year strategic planning exercise for the college, defining the key initiatives that took CSLA to national and international prominence in education and research through highly ranked mathematics and physics programs. Responding to industry demands and building on evolving research strengths at the university, we also opted to make human, programmatic, and physical investments in the new Department of Biological Sciences, created under the first plan, while expanding the presence of life sciences in all other departments as a unifying theme for the college. These sustainable growth initiatives coincided with increased student diversity and academic quality, alongside an intensified commitment to the core mission of delivering a superior general education curriculum in mathematics, the sciences, and humanities to all NJIT students. CSLA, by then, was a very different college than the one I had moved back to in 2003, and I wanted to continue this work with my CSLA colleagues.

~

It was during this period, in 2011, that my father passed away from a heart attack at the age of seventy-six. He had defied medical expectations for decades, surviving the traumatic head injury caused by the malfunctioning of a hunting rifle in his youth, followed by multiple unsuccessful surgeries in the 1970s and 1980s to reconstruct the significant bone loss in his forehead using synthetic material and to address recurring infections. None were successful. The medical interventions were unable to restore the integrity of the bone to provide protection, and in fact the opening in the forehead grew larger with each procedure, leaving a portion of his frontal bone unprotected and permanently compromised.

My father showed remarkable resilience, embracing these challenges and making meaningful contributions in both the personal and professional realms. In fact, when my paternal grandfather sold his home in Beirut in 1976 and shared the proceeds with his children, my father used his portion to establish a successful casual clothing business. My brothers and I were very involved in helping our father run this enterprise, after school and during the summers, until we started to leave the country one after the other. Sami, in particular, was instrumental in expanding the business into the wholesale realm for a period of time before he too left the country. Soon after, my father had to shut down the business because of the continued security deterioration that caused a severe and persistent recession in the country.

Despite undergoing a quadruple coronary artery bypass and suffering from severe heart muscle damage that impaired his heart's ability to pump effectively, my father continued his long-standing habits of smoking and drinking, which ultimately contributed to his declining health. I was present for his funeral, as were all my brothers and a large contingent of family and friends, as he was laid to rest in a new family mausoleum, completed only a short time before his passing. I also returned for the forty-day memorial service, accompanied by my three children.

My father with the ever-present tobacco product in his mouth.

My father, a professional in every sense of the word, was always impeccably dressed, even on the days he did not go to work. He had a keen sense of style, always loving a drink and a cigarette, occasionally swapping his cigarette for a cigar on holidays and special occasions. A detail-oriented person, he was well-read on a range of topics, although politics was his true passion. Every morning, he would buy the newspaper on his way to work, except for Sundays. That was my job. As a young child, I would walk a couple of blocks to the neighborhood bookstore, Librairie Sayah, and carry back what felt like the thickest publication I had ever seen. The Sunday edition of the *An-Nahar* newspaper, with its many supplements, was a heavy responsibility I carried for him. Those Sundays fostered a welcome bond between us, with me sitting next to him as he read the newspaper over morning coffee and then handing me the sections he was done with to read myself. Toward the end of his life, as his health deteriorated, this changed. He stopped reading, letting go of the habits that once defined his routine. But he never stopped wearing his suit and tie each Sunday, even though he no longer left the house. It was as though that small act of maintaining his appearance was one last thread of order, a way to preserve the dignity and control he had always upheld.

After my father died, my mother gave me and my brothers access to his closet, and each of us gravitated toward something different. My interest was in his large collection of ties, which I brought home with me and shared with my two boys. Over time, I became deeply attached to these ties, so much so that I taught myself the art of tailoring. I learned how to unravel the ties back to their basic parts, allowing me to rebuild them in new styles, wider or narrower, depending on the prevailing fashion in order to prolong their usefulness. In doing so, I found not just a way to preserve a piece of my father's legacy, but a means of reshaping it into something that still felt relevant, something I could pass down to my own children. Exchanging ties with my boys became a tradition in its own right, one that connected three generations through a special memory.

Starting in 2011, with my mother now living alone, I began visiting more often, multiple times a year, and spending all my time there with her. We found comfort in speaking and reminiscing about our lives, often very late in the evenings and into the early morning hours. It was during those quiet hours that I began to write down some of the stories and interesting things my mother would say that I found applicable to my daily life. I had heard many of these stories in my earlier years but never thought to record them in writing before. Now I have.

My mother, in deep thoughts.

I enjoyed my tradition of making several trips each year to Lebanon to spend time with my mother. Sometimes I traveled alone, and other times with one or more of my children. I was also able to maximize my visits with my mother by carving time out of my business travels to that part of the world to make time to be with her.

My mother with Matthew and Rebecca.

My mother with Andrew and Rebecca.

Eventually, with the travel restrictions caused by the COVID-19 pandemic, our visitation schedule was disrupted. Luckily, I had been in Lebanon to see my mother multiple times right before the pandemic hit in 2019, including when I made an official visit to the American University of Beirut in the spring and then again in the summer with Matthew and Rebecca.

As COVID-19 spread, I urged my mother to avoid crowded areas and unnecessary social interactions out of concern for her health and safety. This was incredibly difficult for her, as she was a hospitable person who always enjoyed being with other people. During the pandemic, she found herself alone.

CHAPTER 6

Senior Administration

When Bob Altenkirch left NJIT in 2011 to become president of the University of Alabama in Huntsville, a new interim president for NJIT was appointed in 2011. Joel Bloom, an accomplished K-12 educator and administrator, became our eighth president. Prior to NJIT, he had worked as an administrator in the New York City school system and later as an assistant commissioner in New Jersey's Department of Education. Joel had already been at NJIT since 1990, first serving as associate vice president for academic affairs, under former provost Gary Thomas, subsequently becoming vice president for academic and student services in 1996, and then appointed as the first dean for the Albert Dorman Honors College in 1998.

During that time, a relatively new provost, Ian Gatley, distinguished professor of physics, had been recruited by Bob. I remained as dean of CSLA and involved in a number of university-wide initiatives, including actively participating in the development and implementation of institutional strategic planning, expanding professional education, and representing the administration in employment collective bargaining. I was also serving as a co-chair of the NJIT Self-Study Steering Committee in preparation for the university's Middle States Commission on Higher Education re-accreditation in 2012. This role further honed my strategic abilities.

Indeed, many of the strategies that led to the university's successful re-accreditation in 2012 were aligned with CSLA's planning, including expanding enrollment, strengthening students' profile, promoting assessment, and assuring student success.

It did not take long before a message from President Bloom arrived, inviting me to a dinner meeting at an off-campus location. It was not difficult for me to anticipate the nature of the conversation. That evening, I was asked to consider an offer to join the leadership team as a senior vice president working exclusively on the presidential agenda. The president had already communicated to the community his intentions to focus externally on important and pressing matters of visibility, fundraising, and government relations on behalf of NJIT. He envisioned this role as akin to a chief operating officer, requiring someone with deep knowledge of the university, its needs, and its human assets. I asked for some time to speak with Maura and think about my fit for this new role.

By now, I had already turned down two opportunities to consider taking on greater responsibilities at NJIT, and it had been nearly a decade since I became CSLA's dean. My primary reason for not considering new opportunities, my family, was now different. Matthew was already in medical school, Andrew was midway through college, and Rebecca was making her way through the last year of high school. After some deliberations with Maura, we both thought that we were close enough to the milestone we had set for my continued grounding in the dean position. Similarly, we felt that CSLA had already been put on a strong foundation, ready for its next leader. Therefore, we concluded that I was free to make whatever decision regarding my next professional role at NJIT that I felt was right for me and for the university.

Although I still wanted time to consider this invitation, the president soon requested a follow-up meeting. He shared with me that he had been thinking about our earlier conversation, and he now had a clearer picture of what was needed for our university at this stage. He confided that he had decided to appoint a new provost, who would serve as chief academic officer and would also function as a chief operating officer. Given my strong academic profile and my proven leadership at the university, especially in successfully working with members of our university community toward a common goal, he would like me to be that person.

The role of the provost and senior vice president for academic affairs, as the title was then, was to focus solely on academic matters. Having multiple senior vice presidents leading in a number of other university functions often caused some confusion about the provost's seniority, and sometimes tension arose among those who held senior titles. The president's suggestion for a change appealed to me. I quickly realized the opportunity to be able to put academics back at the top of the university's priority list. I also realized that this was exactly the type of structure needed for anyone at the helm of academic affairs to succeed. I knew this firsthand: during the decade I served as dean of CSLA, I reported to six different provosts—three permanent and three interim.

Shortly after my follow-up meeting with him, I informed Joel that I looked forward to the partnership on behalf of NJIT. Having shied away from pursuing such an opportunity twice before, it seemed that the third time was the charm. I did not negotiate any aspect of this assignment other than a request that a formal search process be conducted, as specified in our faculty handbook, in which I would become a candidate, along with others.

President Bloom assumed his permanent role in 2012, with the Board of Trustees' approval but without the customary search process that was attendant to the shared governance initiative that was, at that point, in its early planning stages at our university. Given my history and relations at the university, especially with the faculty, I wanted my appointment, should I be the person chosen for the position, to usher in a new and harmonious era for NJIT. Thus, competing for the position according to the process outlined in the faculty handbook was a non-negotiable request of mine. That is exactly what happened.

On January 14, 2013, three decades to the day after I arrived in the United States, I assumed the new role of provost and senior vice president for academic affairs on an interim basis, as agreed, while a national search was being conducted. Six months later, with the conclusion of this search, I assumed the position formally under the new title of provost and senior executive vice president. I served in that role for a decade. While overseeing academic affairs made up a significant component of this position, it also now encompassed expansive responsibilities in overseeing other key functions at the university.

In life, we often encounter moments of success, recognition, and praise. These external validations can be powerful, shaping the way we view ourselves and our place in the world. However, it is important to recognize that the way we internalize these affirmations is largely dependent on the value we assign to them and the space we allow for them in our own minds. Without self-awareness, intellectual humility, and emotional maturity, these moments can easily inflate our sense of self-importance and create space for external validation that shapes our identity, typically not for the better.

I vividly recall the full-day interview for the provost position I had with my colleagues at NJIT and members of the community at large. It was nothing short of exhilarating and gratifying. The day-long event culminated with a meeting in one of NJIT's largest auditoriums. It was packed—standing room only. Other finalists, external to the university, had been given the same opportunity but their sessions were attended by only a very small number of individuals. The NJIT community was kind to me by coming out in full force to support me, and I was humbled by their presence. I remember returning home that day, very late in the evening, and both Maura and I were really tired and ready to go to bed. As we were both falling asleep, I touched Maura to see if she was still awake, or more likely to awaken her, and said: "Maura, if any of what we saw today goes to my head, will you please let me know?" She characteristically replied: "Yes, but I do not think this will happen. Go to sleep now."

~

A division of labor that put the right person in the right role at the right time yielded a recognized transformation at NJIT. Joel and I brought different skill sets and complementary strengths to the leadership team. Sharing the leadership role effectively allowed us to cover a broader range of challenges. The president, drawing on his earlier state government experience, excelled at external relations at the executive and legislative levels of state government. I excelled in academic strategic vision, organizational long-term planning, operational execution, and team coordination. Often, the president called on me to participate in governmental and philanthropic activities, which I enjoyed and was good at.

This complementarity allowed us to balance the high-level presidential direction with my strategic thinking and practical on-ground implementation, fostering a more dynamic, well-rounded approach to running the university. Our collaboration also promoted diverse perspectives and contrasting management styles, leading to better decision-making, more innovative solutions, and community satisfaction.

In 2018, it was a pleasure for me to welcome and introduce Governor Phil Murphy to NJIT where he named some of his new cabinet members.

My expanded dual role as provost and senior executive vice president necessitated some administrative reorganizations at the top of the organizational hierarchy, placing additional university-wide administrative and resource management accountabilities in the provost's domain, consistent with the newly added title of senior executive vice president. In addition to reporting to the president, all senior vice presidents, vice presidents, and chief officers had another reporting line to me. This structure allowed me to enjoy a close working relationship with every one of these colleagues, giving me additional opportunities to learn, collaborate, mentor, and better understand the interconnection of various university units as well as impact their own growth and development. Just as important, this management structure and the relations it afforded gave me the opportunity and the ethical influence to advocate for the academic mission of the university. These efforts were demanding and time-intensive, and I am incredibly proud of what we have accomplished together across all domains.

Soon after, another administrative reorganization resulted in the elimination of one senior vice president position, one charged with overseeing research, a function that was then moved under my purview. Through this change, I was able to position research at the very center of academic life at NJIT. It resulted in a full integration of our research enterprise—from the recruitment of new faculty and the creation of interdisciplinary research hubs to the proliferation of research opportunities for our graduate and undergraduate students, to fostering collaborations that led to groundbreaking new ideas and inventions that advance society.

With research now reporting directly to me, I was able to promote scholarly collaborations among our schools and colleges, working with the deans to empower our faculty to pursue major funding toward solving cross-disciplinary problems beyond the capabilities of a single researcher. I also strengthened our relationships with our neighbors, Rutgers-Newark and Rutgers Biomedical and Health Sciences, resulting in much stronger cooperation in the area of biological and life sciences. Together, we developed articulated academic programs, joint research groups, grant proposals, and coordinated hires. With all this, there was a feeling on our campus that the transitioning of NJIT from a primarily teaching-focused university to a fully research-intensive one, a goal that was decades in the making and first envisioned by President Fenster and advanced by Provost Thomas, was now truly complete.

Yet another reorganization followed, this time eliminating a vice president position and placing academic and student support services under my domain. This reunification of functions with academic affairs enabled a holistic view of the entire student life cycle. Starting with recruiting and admissions, proceeding through registration, financial aid, advising, tutoring, technology for teaching and learning, and concluding with career development, I was able to impact the inner workings of these offices, leading to consistent and sustained improvements in student outcomes. Other student support services including the Center for Pre-College Programs, the Office of Global Initiatives, the Office of Digital Learning, and Undergraduate Studies were also integrated under the provost's purview. This allowed for a comprehensive understanding of the student experience from start to finish.

One of the most consequential collaborations for the university and its students was the close working and personal relationship I developed with the senior vice president in charge of facilities and infrastructure, Andrew Christ, and the senior vice president in charge of budget and finance, Edward Bishof. Together, we supported the implementation of a faculty and campus renewal plan, a key component of the *2020 Vision* strategic plan, that yielded ambitious results through strategic faculty hires and upgrades of our teaching and learning spaces, research laboratories, and core facilities. These efforts and accompanying investments have paid, and continue to pay, handsome dividends in faculty recognition and students' success, and ultimately benefit the entire university community.

As provost, I needed Andrew's and Ed's support to successfully carry out the faculty and campus renewal plan and to demonstrate to prospective faculty that the necessary infrastructure and resources would be in place to support their ambitious and impactful research. At the time, our facilities required substantial improvements and expansions, an effort that had to compete with other major capital projects across the university.

Andrew, a proud NJIT alumnus, was recruited to NJIT in 2014 to oversee the planned construction of a number of facilities and significant renewal of existing structures. Ed, who had been at the university for thirty-three years, serving in various roles, was a good steward of NJIT's resources. He and I had collaborated closely in all of our prior roles at the university. Both Ed and Andrew fully recognized that the success of the faculty renewal initiative, as well as the broader strategic plan and its focus on attracting high-caliber students and faculty, depended on targeted and thoughtful investments in our academic environment. They worked closely and diligently with me to ensure that academic priorities were not only clearly articulated but also placed at the forefront of institutional decision-making and funding decisions. Their commitment and collaboration were instrumental in advancing our shared goals.

~

Innovation and visionary thinking, qualities of consequential importance in academia, require careful strategic planning, ongoing assessment and, most essentially, collaboration. To produce fundamental changes at our university, I worked to bring together and motivate key stakeholders to enact ambitious yet well thought out efforts. My exposure to strategic thinking had been honed and practiced over a long period of time. In fact, my first exposure to strategic planning occurred when I was associate dean for the College of Computing, immediately after its creation, a role in which I led the development of a five-year strategic plan that involved identifying priorities, implementation details, and performance metrics for this new college. I similarly engaged in two cycles of intensive strategic planning immediately after assuming the deanship of CSLA, with both of these strategic plans profoundly influencing the college's trajectory in essentially every respect.

Shortly after becoming provost, I quickly began the creation of the long-awaited *NJIT Academic Plan: 2013–2015*, devoting time and energy to working with faculty, administrators, staff, and students. This work laid the foundation for a new shared governance system that I facilitated after it was stalled in 2012, and I oversaw the implementation of an ambitious faculty hiring plan. In addition to my own personal involvement, every one of these efforts required the forging of partnerships and the formation of teams to carry out significant tasks successfully and within a short period of time.

Soon after becoming provost, the president also asked me to develop a major proposal in response to New Jersey's Building Our Future Bond Act. Using the same model of collaboration I had always found so important, I worked extensively with a small group of NJIT colleagues to craft a compelling case for funding the renovation of the Central King Building. Our proposal was awarded $86 million, the largest amount given to any college/university for a single project by this state fund. This was a momentous win for our university. The grant enabled us to renovate the former Newark Central High School, located at the heart of our campus, to its former glory and beauty as an act of appreciation on the university's part to Newark, the city we proudly call home.

The *Academic Plan* exercise and the Central King Building proposal highlighted my greatest strength—team building. Throughout my career, I brought together individuals with complementary skills and differing viewpoints, including those who disagreed with me. I have long believed that solutions developed in isolation rarely succeed. While I motivated and worked with these teams, I also respected each individual's knowledge and skills, allowing the most capable person to take the lead. This has been essential to my career success thus far.

A most momentous undertaking came in 2014, when we began the development of a comprehensive university strategic plan, *2020 Vision*. While led by me, this effort involved the active participation of more than two hundred members of the university community. The outcomes of our five priorities—Students, Learning, Research, Community, and Investment—were documented through fifty key performance indicators that offered strong evidence of the transformation that occurred on our campus as a result of that plan's implementation.

In the area of Students, I understood the importance of moving our application process to the common app to give us a global presence. This change led to an immediate and significant increase in applications, enabling thoughtful selectivity. Even more importantly, our continuing success led to an increase in reputation and recognition, resulting in students and parents viewing NJIT in a new and more favorable light. As a result, by the conclusion of the *2020 Vision* strategic plan, we were receiving three times the number of applications we received at our starting point in 2015. The gains in applications yielded a corresponding growth in the enrollment of highly qualified and diverse students. The improved student profile, combined with expanded student services, including the creation of distributed tutoring centers in key departments, resulted in significant increases in retention and graduation rates. Such performance enabled us to achieve a top 100 national university status.

Faculty are an essential component in the equation of student success. Having experienced a long period without any significant investment in faculty renewal, my senior vice provost colleagues and I developed an ambitious faculty hiring plan as part of *2020 Vision*. The investment in faculty driven by our strategic plan was critical to our academic mission, but I also understood the correlation between faculty renewal and research success. These efforts culminated in NJIT being designated, for the first time, as a Carnegie R1 (Very High Research Activity) institution, the highest designation awarded.

Together, these outcomes—student success, faculty renewal, and research growth—were directly responsible for NJIT's strong performance in the many prestigious national and international rankings. It gives me satisfaction that the faculty renewal initiative under *2020 Vision* resulted in a large segment of our faculty body being recruited and hired during my time as provost, more than half of the total by the conclusion of the plan.

~

My memory of this time runs on two paths, the academic success tempered by personal loss. Our distress began on January 12, 2016, when I received word about my brother Sami's passing from a heart attack, just days before he was to wrap up a major construction project in Morocco on behalf of his employer. That same night, my brother Roland, who lives in Montreal, and I met in Paris and we flew together to Morocco to bring Sami home to Lebanon. After arriving in Casablanca, we faced a grueling journey, travelling for hours to the location where Sami had been staying as the project was being built. There, we were met and supported by so many kind and special people from Sami's company who were visibly as distraught as we were and also as fond of him as we are. It was truly comforting to see that everyone we met who knew Sami loved him.

Sami had been in Ephran, Morocco, for a short period, less than two weeks, and had only a few days left before returning to Qatar. Prior to this trip, Sami was assigned full-time to oversee this project, the building of the winter ski retreat for the ruling family of Qatar. Once the project was completed, he was recalled to Qatar and promoted to deputy CEO of his company, a large organization with more than 60,000 employees. This final trip was to conclude some final finishing details before the building was delivered to its new occupant.

Sami's passing away in a distant land was heartbreaking, and completing the paperwork to bring him home was complex and frustrating to say the least. However, we were eternally appreciative to receive the help of many people, particularly the company officials and Sami's colleagues, who worked with us in Morocco to conclude the transfer process in record time. We had been warned that the normal procedure could extend into many days, and possibly weeks, depending on the circumstances. But Roland and

I were determined to bring our brother home as quickly as possible. Sami's colleagues and friends were also determined to help us accomplish our goal. Our mother, Sami's wife, Jacqueline, and his children, Stephanie and Jason, were all waiting at my family's home for his return to Jbeil and to see him one last time.

The task of bringing Sami home required coordination between many people who worked beyond their normal hours and offices that remained open beyond their normal schedules, located in different cities, to conclude all necessary certifications and documentation. The Lebanese chargé d'affaires in Rabat was amazingly helpful. We were proud that Lebanon is so well represented in Morocco and that the Lebanese located there have her as a strong advocate. One of the many phone calls she made resulted in us receiving our last signature to take Sami home, at 10:00 pm on the second day of our journey.

Thus, two days after we arrived in Morocco, we left for Lebanon with our brother Sami on the same airplane. We were met at Beirut Airport by a number of distraught family members and friends and again at home in Jbeil, where a massive crowd of family and friends was assembled. The next day, Sami was laid to rest in the family's burial site near our father. Among the five siblings, more than anyone else, Sami had enjoyed a special connection with our father, not only in their shared birthday date but also in many of their personal traits: generous spirits, big hearts, zest for life, and, yes, fondness for drinking and smoking. In a poignant twist of fate, both passed away from heart-related conditions. It felt deeply symbolic that Sami was the first to join our father in the family mausoleum in Jbeil, as if they were continuing their journey together.

~

While none were as personally devastating as Sami's death, there were some truly difficult times too during my decade as provost and senior executive vice president. One stands out in particular: the COVID-19 pandemic. In spring 2020, like the rest of the higher education enterprise, and the rest of the world for that matter, the global pandemic forced NJIT to move to remote operations, including instruction, research, and business functions. Fortunately, our deliberate investments in instructional technology and increased digital capabilities across our campus, made as part of the *2020 Vision* strategic plan, accelerated in the period immediately after the start of the pandemic, proved both wise and timely. In March of 2020, NJIT instantaneously and seamlessly shifted to converged learning, a term we had coined earlier, in which instructors taught synchronously using their office or home computers with students also joining regardless of their location. Despite the unforeseen nature of this transition, the remote converged learning format worked remarkably well given its sudden implementation. I had envisioned the converged learning model, which I first detailed in a 2013 white paper posted on the provost's website, as a means of ensuring the accessibility of an NJIT education. With a minimum of equipment (laptop, microphone, and camera), all of our instructors were teaching and interacting with their students ten days after the official move to remote operations. For instructors and students lacking the necessary technologies, the university provided devices to facilitate the sudden transition to remote converged learning.

At the same time, guided by a comprehensive *Pandemic Recovery Plan*, developed and implemented by my colleagues and me, the university began to prepare for a return to campus by the fall of 2020. We used converged learning as a means to support appropriate social distancing while still providing students with on-campus, face-to-face experiences. The converged format provided a flexibility that was well suited to the uncertainty caused by the pandemic. It allowed students to determine their preferred method of attendance: for those students anxious to return, or come to campus, converged learning provided the option to attend class in person or join from the library, residence halls, or other study spaces made available by the university or chosen for themselves. Meanwhile, students concerned about returning too soon could continue to participate remotely, always with the option to switch to in-person attendance at any time. Thanks to our plan and this flexible approach, NJIT was able to resume near-normal operations much sooner than many peer institutions that remained fully remote for an extended time.

Our University Communications group took this picture of Maura and me in 2020 during the COVID-19 pandemic as part of an outreach message of hope and resilience to our community. We are a proud NJIT family, with every member holding at least one degree from the university.

~

One of the most pivotal decisions made during my tenure in academic leadership was the institution of a collaborative governance framework that the university functioned under for a decade while I served as provost. Resuming the stalled discussions toward forming a shared governance model, and ultimately adopting it, was one of my first tasks as provost. This model, which remained in place subsequent to my departure, capitalized on our complementary strengths, resulting in a partnership that contributed directly to the university's transformation and increased recognition.

President Bloom came to NJIT after a successful career in the education sector, both at the school district level and in state government. His strength lay in his ability to connect with external stakeholders—politicians, donors, alumni, and other leaders in both the private and public sectors. He was effective in forming relationships that opened doors, attracted funding, and raised NJIT's reputation in our state and nationally. His time away from the campus allowed him to focus on strategic partnerships that positioned our university as a visible leader in higher education.

In contrast, my career has been firmly rooted in collegiate education. My career gave me a solid understanding of the internal workings of the university, the challenges and opportunities facing both students and faculty, and the necessary incentives and mechanisms for academic advancement. I understood the nuances of curriculum design and delivery, the importance of faculty recruitment and development, and the need to cultivate and support a research-driven academic culture.

Our partnership was built on a purposeful division of labor that allowed us to focus on our respective strengths while supporting the other's efforts. The president's external focus, which included increasing the university's visibility, securing philanthropic investments, and forging new institutional alliances, was complemented by my internal focus on fostering academic excellence, nurturing student and faculty success, and driving the intellectual maturity of the institution. This division of responsibilities was not simply a practical arrangement; it was a conscious strategy to ensure that both the internal and external dimensions of the university were attended to with the necessary focus and expertise.

Together, we formed a complementary leadership that was able to propel the university forward. With our combined efforts,

NJIT not only gained recognition as an R1 institution but also ascended to the top 100 ranks in national university standings. I led the academic transformation, ensuring that the university's research capacity expanded and that students and faculty were supported in ways that facilitated both their academic success and personal development. This internal focus fostered a thriving, vibrant academic community that would attract high-caliber students and faculty, and eventually external recognition. At the same time, the president's focus on building relationships and securing resources was essential to my leadership in academic affairs, ensuring that the university's mission was realized in tangible ways. Our model of leadership, balancing external visibility with internal excellence, enabled the university to flourish as both a national and international powerhouse.

~

There was also a complementary arrangement, a division of labor within academic affairs, that proved equally instrumental to our success. When I accepted the position of provost, I fully understood the magnitude of the responsibility and the importance of assembling a leadership team that not only shared my philosophy and work ethic but also embraced my vision of re-centering academic affairs at the heart of the university's mission. Drawing on my long-standing experience at the institution, I already had a sense of who among my colleagues I could count on to help advance this ambitious agenda. Given our ambitious strategic priorities, I also expected that new colleagues from outside the university would be attracted to NJIT for leadership roles.

At the top of the list was Basil Baltzis, then serving as interim dean for Newark College of Engineering, with a long history at NJIT. His sustained record of accomplishments and his unwavering reputation for integrity and dedication to the university made him an ideal partner. I knew the path ahead would be both demanding and transformative, and Basil had the endurance, insight, and collegial spirit necessary to navigate it. Most importantly, he was someone I could trust, an individual with whom I could work closely and seamlessly. His preference would have been to remain at the helm in NCE, where he was already implementing his vision for a harmonious education and research agenda. However, after a brief conversation, we both concluded that his energy would have more impact university-wide.

I was fortunate that Basil accepted my invitation to join the leadership team as senior vice provost for academic affairs and student services, a role he held until we both transitioned back to our faculty positions. Throughout our time in the provost's office, we worked in close partnership, grounded in shared professional values and mutual respect. Our collaboration was not only highly productive, but also deeply rewarding, evolving into a lasting friendship that continues to this day. His integrity, wisdom, commitment, and tireless work made a lasting impact, and I remain deeply grateful for his partnership during a pivotal chapter in the university's evolution. One of his important and visible legacies was founding and leading NJIT's Institute for Teaching Excellence. The creation of ITE sent a message of our sincere commitment to quality teaching and learning, even as we pressed on intensely toward a strong research university.

During my decade of service in academic affairs, working with fellow faculty and administration, gradually and as positions became available, I had the opportunity and pleasure to eventually place new leaders, from within as well as from outside the university, at the helm of all NJIT colleges and schools. Their efforts jointly with the efforts of many other individuals on our campus created the ripe conditions for the successes our university has enjoyed.

In 2014, Newark College of Engineering, our flagship college, led our search for leaders. Engineering, where our roots are, continues to define our university, with NCE itself being recognized as a brand in similar ways to NJIT. I was fortunate to entice a visionary disruptor, and an accomplished academic, Moshe Kam, who brought both energy and vision for the future of engineering to NJIT but also beyond. Dean Kam joined us in 2014. Coming from outside the university, Moshe brought fresh momentum to NCE, along with international visibility and a distinguished reputation in the global engineering community, which significantly enhanced our institution's profile.

Under Moshe's dedicated leadership, NCE rose into the top 100 national rankings, an achievement that speaks to his strategic insight and commitment to excellence. Yet, beyond rankings and accolades, what distinguished Moshe the most was his collegiality, professionalism, and remarkable humility. These qualities made him not only an effective dean, but also an outstanding member of our university community, enriching our collective work with both expertise and grace. I worked very closely with Moshe on NCE's faculty renewal plan and consistently appreciated his thoroughness, wisdom, and determination in pursuing individuals of the highest caliber for his college. He used the same thoughtful approach in expanding his college's enrollment. To this day, I often cite him as a role model for others.

After I had completed a decade of service as dean of the College of Science and Liberal Arts and then transitioned to the role of provost, the college continued to hold a special place in my heart for many reasons. I felt that CSLA was now ready for its next leader, who would bring vision and ideas toward new heights, especially given the strong foundation and elevated standing we had worked hard to achieve. It was important to me that we clearly communicate to all prospective leaders that this was not merely a continuation but a unique opportunity to build upon that foundation, aiming even higher to advance the college to new levels of excellence.

I was pleased when, also in 2014, we finally recruited a successor for me as Dean of CSLA, Kevin Belfield, who has successfully sustained the college's trajectory of strength and achievement. Dean Belfield joined us in 2014 and has led with integrity, serving as a fair and principled administrator, a thoughtful academic leader, and an active researcher. Remarkably, Kevin continues to maintain a fully staffed and productive research laboratory, mentoring a substantial number of PhD students and postdoctoral fellows. His ability to balance administrative leadership with scholarly excellence is both rare and commendable.

Also, in 2014, Reggie Caudill was appointed dean of the School of Management, initially in an interim capacity, and later confirmed as permanent dean with strong support from the faculty. A professor in NJIT's Department of Mechanical and Industrial Engineering and its former chair, Dean Caudill was a well-established member of the faculty with a track record of research achievements on campus. Under his leadership, the management faculty developed the school's first academic plan, which served as a strategic roadmap for their future goals and objectives. This plan offered a differentiated character for the school's programs, capitalizing on the strengths of engineering, computing, and the sciences, and aligning them with the broader priorities of the *2020 Vision* strategic plan. Reggie's leadership, and the faculty's efforts, led to significant evolution in the school. This resulted in the creation of the Leir Research Institute and the development of their first ever PhD program, which enabled the management faculty to significantly expand their sponsored research portfolio.

Three years later, in 2017, I had the opportunity to make another pivotal leadership appointment, this time at the helm of one of the university's most dynamic and strategically important colleges. In 2017, we welcomed Craig Gotsman, a distinguished computer scientist, as dean of the College of Computing. Recruiting Dean Gotsman was both challenging and immensely rewarding. A renowned scholar, inventor, and experienced administrator, Craig brought with him a stellar record of achievement, having held positions at some of the world's leading universities. Understandably, he sought clear assurances that he would have the support and autonomy necessary to advance his ambitious agenda and make a meaningful impact. Craig's arrival marked a significant moment for all of NJIT's computing disciplines and aligned with our broader strategic priorities.

After a series of thoughtful conversations, it became clear to me that his vision held promise toward enabling us to achieve our institutional goals. I had no hesitation in offering my full support. Craig not only fulfilled his commitments, he exceeded them. Under his leadership, the college was transformed: energized, strategically organized, significantly expanded, and nationally ranked. Craig became the enterprising dean everyone had envisioned for the College of Computing when it was established in 2001 under the leadership of Provost Van Buskirk. Notable achievements during Craig's tenure include unprecedented enrollment growth, the establishment of a satellite facility in Jersey City, a premier hub for information technology and innovation that now hosts academic programs, and the founding of the Institute for Future Technologies. These accomplishments have further elevated our university's national and international reputation in computing and beyond.

More appointments followed in the remaining schools and colleges. In 2017, Louis Hamilton, a medieval historian whose research focuses on the High Middle Ages in Italy, particularly Rome, was appointed dean of the Albert Dorman Honors College. This is an important college at NJIT, providing a rigorous and intellectually stimulating environment for high-achieving students across all disciplines, attracting accomplished scholars from both New Jersey and the nation. Dean Hamilton quickly implemented new educational and research initiatives designed to enhance the academic experience for our students and to prepare them as transformational leaders in both their professional and personal communities. Under Louis' leadership, the college has seen significant success in enabling students to earn prestigious national awards, including National Science Foundation grants, Fulbright scholarships, Goldwater scholarships, and other notable academic exchange opportunities.

Following his outstanding career in both engineering and management, Reggie Caudill announced his retirement. In 2019, this leadership transition allowed us to appoint Oya Tukel, an accomplished researcher in operations and supply chain management, as the new dean of the School of Management. Dean Tukel brought with her innovative ideas and a strategic vision aimed at expanding the visibility of the school through community engagement, interdisciplinary research initiatives, and expanded student enrollment. Notably, Oya spearheaded the development of a new undergraduate program in Financial Technology and fostered strong connections with industry and government partners. These initiatives, and her active involvement at the state level, have greatly contributed to NJIT's growing prominence in management education and research.

After a distinguished tenure of over twenty-five years at the helm of NJIT's College of Architecture and Design, Dean Urs Gauchat transitioned into retirement. I recognized that identifying the right successor to lead this college would be a complex and challenging task. However, the remarkable transformation under Urs' leadership made the college an exceptionally attractive opportunity for potential candidates. After a thorough search, we were fortunate to welcome Branko Kolarevic as the new dean. Dean Kolarevic joined the college in 2019 and brought with him a wealth of experience as a leader in his field, with an outstanding record of accomplishments in education, research, and administration. One of the first things Branko did was to expand the scope of the PhD program in Urban Systems, offered by his college, beyond its original social science roots to include a strong presence in computational design methods, which has increased the program's appeal to both faculty and students. Unfortunately, the onset of the COVID-19 pandemic, along with its associated restrictions, disrupted and delayed many of the ambitious initiatives that Branko had envisioned for the college's future. Branko's untimely passing in 2026 was a significant loss to his family, our university, and the global architecture community.

I was incredibly fortunate to lead academic affairs as a partnership with dedicated and highly skilled individuals, each of whom contributed directly to our success. However, as is often the case with successful organizations, there is always one person whose behind-the-scenes work truly impacts progress. Peggy Kenrick, the director of administration in my office, was that person. The importance of her role could not be overstated. Peggy's ability to coordinate, manage, and follow through on the many details of our work was nothing short of extraordinary. None of our key accomplishments, for example in strategic planning and faculty renewal, would have been possible without her relentless commitment and expert navigation of complex tasks.

Peggy was a quick thinker with a firm yet fair demeanor, and the ability to speak with authority and sensitivity. She juggled a large number of visible projects, each demanding precision and clarity, and made it look effortless. No matter the challenge, Peggy approached every situation with integrity, honesty, and a sense of dedication to ensure that things got done on time and right. Without her vigilance and insight, our success would simply not have been possible.

These leaders, and others at all levels and in all areas of the university, particularly within the greater scope of academic affairs, and colleagues too numerous to name, became the engine that propelled our university to greater heights over the next several years.

Their energy continues to garner us recognition and accolades. They deserve sincere recognition and praise for their commitment and dedication.

~

Sadly, in 2020, amid the height of the pandemic, my mother was diagnosed with an aggressive, fast-moving metastatic breast cancer. She passed away just six weeks later, at the age of eighty-two. Upon receiving the details of her diagnosis, I immediately flew to Lebanon, traveling from Newark to Beirut through Europe on nearly empty planes because of the pandemic, to be with her during her hospitalization. This was such an unusually difficult time, as the pandemic had already reshaped our lives in unexpected and profound ways. Public health restrictions meant that face masks became ubiquitous, physical interactions were limited, and hospital visits were controlled and generally limited to next of kin. During one of my daily visits to the hospital, I sat by my mother's bedside as she, ever resilient, sought to reassure me that everything would be all right. While we both held onto hope, we also understood the harsh reality of the illness she was facing.

I returned briefly to the United States when my brothers returned to be with her. Bassam came back from Australia and Roland from Canada to be with our mother during her short hospital stay. Wadih, who had never left Lebanon, was always with us and by our mother's side. I traveled back to Lebanon again on the day she passed and was there for her funeral. On October 26, 2020, she joined our father and our brother Sami in the family's mausoleum. May her stories be red flags, silent signals summoned from memory, sent to summon us home.

One year before she succumbed to a vicious and fast spreading cancer, my mother seemed happy and vigorous.

I take comfort in the fact that I was able to visit my mother routinely, frequently with Maura and our children, which brought her great joy. One of the things she cherished most was the time Rebecca spent with her alone. Over the course of two consecutive summers, before the pandemic, Rebecca lived with my mother, for eight weeks each time, while conducting research at the Lebanese American University as part of her graduate studies. This time together allowed them to form a meaningful bond. Rebecca had the invaluable opportunity to learn how to prepare my mother's traditional Lebanese dishes and to practice the spoken Lebanese language she had been studying independently. It was an enriching experience for both of them, one that I know my mother and Rebecca truly appreciated.

My mother insisted on bringing Rebecca back to Beirut Airport after Rebecca's lengthy summer visits with her.

~

Immediately after my mother's passing, I was presented with a significant personal and professional challenge that tested my core beliefs. As I have shared, throughout my life, and particularly in my career, I have consistently adhered to the principle that everything, in the end, will fall into place as it should. This mindset has also guided me to focus only on the elements within my control, while accepting that there are aspects beyond my influence.

In 2020, our university's president announced his plan to retire within two years, and the NJIT Board of Trustees signaled their intent to begin a search for a new leader. The new president would be appointed by July 1, 2022. Given my extensive history with the university, I felt both prepared and ready to be part of this leadership transition. It was my wish to contribute my vision for the next chapter of the university, one that would build on the solid foundation we had established over the past decade and would continue the positive momentum we had achieved.

I believed my career had positioned me well for this leadership role, and I was encouraged by the conversations the Board and university leadership had with me. Shortly after the president's announcement, both the Board Chair at the time and the president of the university met with me to discuss a transition plan. They expressed their desire to effect a transition that would begin to immediately involve me more deeply in external university functions, such as government relations and fundraising, areas which had been exclusively in the president's domain. While these areas were not part of my day-to-day responsibilities as provost, I had experience and success in these functions from prior roles, specifically as dean, but also in my role as provost at the invitation of the president. This was a continuation of a discussion that began a year earlier with the Board Chair while on a business trip. He outlined his expectations for how the search would unfold and cited my strength as a candidate. I was excited to have the opportunity to learn more and contribute further.

During this time, I also received significant support from key Board members and from both internal and external stakeholders, who expressed excitement about the transition and confidence in my ability to lead the university forward as its president. As I had always done, I focused on the elements I could control—be prepared, be ready, be myself.

Nonetheless, before the search process began, a new chair for the Board was selected in 2020. Ultimately, both the Board and I diverged. While this was a difficult period in my career, I chose to remain at the university. The period that followed was challenging, especially for my family, but I remained committed to the university's success. Also, I was deeply moved by the overwhelming support I received from both the university community and from others beyond our campus boundaries who expressed their feelings of great surprise and deep disappointment.

My decision to step away from my role as provost and senior executive vice president was purposefully made, separately, a year prior to the start of the presidential search. My return to my academic roots has allowed me to refocus and devote more time to the work I am most passionate about: teaching, research, mentoring junior faculty, and guiding PhD students who are the next generation of researchers to build their own successful careers. My colleagues and peers have commended my approach to dealing with the ramifications of this outcome, particularly my decision to stay at NJIT, where members of the community at all levels of the organization have continued to call on me for counsel and guidance.

My transition from administration back to faculty has brought me immense fulfillment and satisfaction. While things did not unfold exactly as I had hoped, I have come to realize that even when life does not go according to plan, it can still fall into place in meaningful and impactful ways.

In an era when academic leadership often requires the sacrifice of one's scholarly identity, my experience challenges the narrative that stepping into administration means permanent detachment from research. I can confirm that it is possible to re-engage with rigorous academic inquiry after a prolonged administrative service, given the right conditions and mindset that facilitate such a transition.

After two decades at the helm of academic administration at NJIT, I had expected my return to the faculty to be a slow reentry into a research world that had long since moved forward without me. What I encountered instead was a profound and almost startling sense of continuity. My research picked up not as a rusty engine groaning to life, but as a long-paused symphony resuming mid-movement.

~

My academic career began with the sense of promise and purpose that often defines the early years of faculty life, including academic and scholarly pursuits. Immersed in my field, I relished the opportunity to engage in inquiry that was both intellectually stimulating and socially meaningful. Early on, I found myself part of a scholarly community that valued not only strong theoretical grounding but also applied innovation.

My research agenda, at its core, bridged the technical, cognitive, societal, and pedagogical dimensions of computing. Throughout my career, I maintained an active research agenda—even while serving in senior university leadership roles, though in a more diminished capacity. My scholarly work explored software engineering and open-source software development, with particular emphasis on learning technologies designed around how people think, acquire knowledge, and collaborate.

Those early years were marked by the exhilarating pace of findings and outcomes. I published consistently, presented at national and international conferences, and began mentoring a small but dedicated research group of graduate and undergraduate students. My work received attention within the field, and I was fortunate to secure grants, awards, and notable recognitions. I was most proud to serve as principal and co-principal investigator on multiple federally funded projects that enabled me to impact the training of graduate students. The satisfaction of building a research program that contributed to ongoing interdisciplinary initiatives was matched only by the gratification of mentoring scholars at all levels of education—an experience that would become central to my professional identity.

During this period, I also devoted time and energy to departmental administration, a strong commitment that came with my appointment to the faculty—serving as associate chair, vice chair, chair, and associate dean from 1997 to 2003. I also became involved in institutional engagement, which, in hindsight, foreshadowed my later leadership path. Yet at the time, the center of gravity in my dual administrative-academic life was rooted in research. The rhythms of writing, revising, and peer review structured my professional life and defined my sense of scholarly belonging.

It is important to emphasize that this was not merely a productive phase in quantitative terms, but a formative one in intellectual terms. The questions I explored during this time, both those I answered and those I left unresolved, continued to shape my thinking, even as the demands of leadership, later on, limited my capacity to pursue them directly. In this way, my early research career laid a foundation that, although it became dormant for some time, proved remarkably resilient.

The trajectory of my academic career shifted dramatically within a relatively short period. The fact that I earned tenure just three years after my appointment to the faculty was a recognition of not only scholarly productivity and teaching excellence but also of an early inclination toward institutional commitment. My promotion to full professor three years later, the subsequent invitation to serve as dean, and my eventual appointment as provost and senior executive vice president were milestones realized in quick succession at an institution that was growing and evolving—a research university environment dedicated to quality education, scholarly achievement, and community engagement. While I had initially imagined administrative responsibilities as an opportunity to make contributions toward improving our university while remaining connected to scholarship, in reality, the demands and expectations of these roles quickly grew into a full intellectual and professional commitment spanning a twenty-year period of continuous and intense academic leadership—impacting research among other areas. I am proud to say, however, that this commitment did not come at the expense of family.

However, the very intensity and scope of these efforts necessarily displaced other aspects of my academic identity. The strategic thinking and actions that helped transform the institution left me little room for sustained scholarly inquiry of my own. While I continued to mentor doctoral students, contribute to academic conversations, and nurture ideas that would eventually reemerge, my primary identity during these years was that of an institutional leader, not an active scholar. And yet, even during the most demanding phases of my administrative career, I never ceased to think like a researcher. I viewed the university as a complex system—one worthy of studying, improving, and advancing—with questions about our unique role in the state of New Jersey, our performance, and our culture in an evolving higher education landscape. This kind of thinking helped me consider and analyze the range of intellectual possibilities when the time came to rejoin the faculty.

~

My decision to return to faculty life was deliberate. I did not take this decision out of fatigue or disillusionment. On the contrary, I had delivered on the promises I made and accomplished the goals I set out to achieve, leaving the university stronger, more energized, and more research-intensive than I had found it.

There was also a personal aspect to my decision. As our family has grown and evolved, so too have our priorities. Our three children, all proud NJIT alumni, had embarked on their own impressive professional journeys. Matthew, a physician, is today actively engaged in an academic medicine career as a radiation oncologist. He married Nisha Narula, a surgeon, on May 16, 2025. Isabelle is their daughter. Andrew has also chosen medicine, launching a career as an oral-cranio-maxillofacial surgeon. He married Michelle Regna, his high school sweetheart and also an NJIT alumna with a graduate degree in information systems, on September 21, 2019. Charles is their son. Rebecca has embraced the world of academia as a university professor in health data science and biostatistics.

People often ask Maura and me what special strategy we used to help our children become successful and productive adults. The honest answer is: we did not follow a special program or formula. What we did was simple but intentional. When our children were young, we were careful not to place undue pressure on them. We did not rush them into preschool or load their schedules with enrichment programs and special academic tracks. Instead, we made it a priority to spend meaningful time together as a family, whether it was our evening dinners or yearly vacations. We were attentive, but not intrusive. We aimed to be available when they signaled they needed guidance or support, while giving them room to grow on their own. A favorite family activity that we have been continually engaged in is fossil excavating.

Given its history, Lebanon has a rich archeological heritage that is very well known and studied. Starting with her first visit, Maura and I have acquired some unique ancient artifacts that we proudly display in our home. However, Lebanon also has an equally rich, but less known, paleontological heritage. This has caught the attention of our children. One of those places is the famous fossil beds of Haqel, in the mountains above Jbeil, which date back about one hundred million years to the Late Cenomanian age. These fossil beds are among the world's most important marine sedimentary deposits of limestone layers that contain preserved fish, crustaceans, and other marine life. On every one of our visits to Lebanon, Joe Khalife, a childhood friend of mine, and I organized an excursion for our two families to a fossil quarry owned by his cousins. Our children have accumulated an impressive collection of fossilized marine life. Incidentally, in addition to being my across-the-street neighbor since we both were born, Joe and I have much in common. He is an avid artifact collector and renowned expert in archeology as well as being a professor of computer science at the Lebanese American University.

Maura perfected her excavation skills at the famous fossil beds of Haqel-Jbeil.

Matthew showing one of the many fossils he dug out.

Andrew is holding a fossil he excavated but seems to be looking for more.

Rebecca resting after digging one of her fossils.

As our children grew older, we encouraged responsibility and character over achievement for its own sake. We hoped that if they developed integrity, empathy, and confidence, the accomplishments would follow naturally. We did not aim to control their path. We just wanted to equip them for it. The rest followed. When they reached college, all opting for NJIT, they chose to engage in meaningful service and serious research experiences. They completed their degrees in three years, at the top of their classes, and moved on to professional and graduate schools with clarity and purpose.

As dean, I received the greatest satisfaction in handing our children their NJIT undergraduate diplomas. Matthew received his in 2011.

Then, as provost, I handed Andrew his NJIT diploma in 2013.

Also as provost, I handed Rebecca her NJIT diploma in 2016.

Maura and I have always taken great pride in the individuals our children have become, and we continue to be inspired by the dedication and purpose with which they approach their lives and careers. Their independence marked a natural transition point for us. Throughout the years, our lives were tightly woven around the responsibilities of parenting, dedication to our respective families, and commitment to our professions, but more so the demands of my own professional functions. While the journey was truly fulfilling and the results gratifying, that pace left little time for one another. As I began to plan the transition to my faculty role, I realized it was time to reclaim some of that space, to be more present with Maura and to give back to the partnership that has supported every stage of our family's journey.

This transition was, in many ways, a return to a prior life I never had a chance to fully live. I was called into administration early in my faculty career, and now I felt the quiet pull back toward teaching and the unfinished scholarly work, the intellectual questions that academic leadership rarely permits. Reintegrating into the academic rhythm required intentionality. I had to recalibrate my schedule, rebuild collaborative networks, and reacquaint myself with a fast-moving computing field.

During my first year back, I spent much of my time in my office reading intensely, acquiring new knowledge in computing that I thought was essential for my successful reentry into the classroom, catching up on research advances in science and technology, and their impact on society, including in historical context. I also reached out to reconnect with former graduate students and mentees, some of whom had become established scholars themselves. Rather than starting from scratch, I found that my scholarly foundation remained robust. My instincts as a researcher had simply been placed in reserve. My return to scholarship was made possible by a personal choice but also by the willingness of students, colleagues, and collaborators to embrace me again as a researcher, for which

I am truly appreciative. Above all, though, I appreciate my ability to reclaim the solitude of reading and shed the burden of constant availability.

I did bring with me one advantage from my former administrative life: I no longer saw research as a narrow disciplinary pursuit. Instead, I now have a panoramic view of academia that is only afforded to senior leadership. I returned to simply resume where I had left off, but what surprised me most was the pace and energy with which my research life resumed.

Undergraduate and graduate students visited my office desiring to learn about my work and seeking mentorship. Ideas I had put aside during my years in administration now came to the forefront. Questions I had pondered from a leadership vantage point guided me in framing a renewed research agenda in computing with a keen interest in having an impact on society. I again began writing with my students again prolifically, and our work was received with both scholarly interest and recognition of its practical relevance. My experience in administration had not distanced me from the academy; it had given me new lenses through which to reexamine it.

I recognize that not all former administrators enjoy such a smooth path. I was fortunate to have the internal drive to reassert my intellectual voice and to benefit from colleagues who welcomed me back as a scholar. In that sense, my experience may be unique, but it affirms that scholarly reengagement is possible and that institutions can cultivate cultures that enable such returns. Viewed in this way, accomplished scholars do not have to shy away from serving in administrative roles as they generally do.

Regarding teaching, despite some initial apprehension, returning to the classroom was equally revitalizing. This transition was made possible by the combination of personal motivation and community support. Maura and some of my colleagues had cautioned me that current and rising generations of learners were different from prior ones I had taught. I was also unsure about what disciplinary subjects I wanted to reclaim for my teaching agenda. While I could have easily returned to topics within my earlier expertise, I opted to heed Maura's advice once again: to learn and teach something new and exciting. I chose to focus on artificial intelligence, with a special interest in philosophy and ethics. My teaching, much like my research, was enriched by the years I spent shaping policy and strategy. I found myself more attuned to the broader context of students' experiences and more deliberate in connecting technological advances to societal realities.

The activation of my research program following two decades in administration was less a restart than a reconnection. The ideas were not new; many had been on my mind for years, concepts I had considered or discussed with colleagues but never had the time to fully pursue. What changed upon returning to the faculty was the availability of time and focus needed to transform those ideas into rigorous scholarly projects. My research agenda has since taken shape and collaborations have emerged organically, including with former doctoral students, now faculty themselves, as well as with peers.

Continuing my commitment to inquiry that impacts society, the technological, philosophical, and ethical implications of artificial intelligence became a unifying theme in both my teaching and research. Also, the impact of AI tools on the cognition of learners is of scholarly interest to me. On the more technical front, my work focuses on the use of machine learning in electronic health records, as well as text and image processing in the domain of medicine. Perhaps most exciting has been my research collaborations with my children on some of these projects. Rebecca and I are co-mentoring undergraduate students working with us on a study that investigates the impact of artificial intelligence on the cognitive system of learners and Matthew is involved with me in the mentoring of doctoral students working with us on medical image processing research.

Doctoral mentorship, too, has taken on new depth. Having guided PhD students both during my leadership years and earlier in my career, I now engage with them as an active researcher, able to model the full cycle of scholarly inquiry. I have found that my administrative experience has sharpened my mentorship, providing a richer understanding of research and institutional contexts in the broader environment in which academic careers unfold.

In returning to research, I did not discard the skills of leadership—I integrated them. Strategic thinking, data-informed decision-making, and team-building are all now part of how I approach scholarly work. In this sense, I am not returning to research as the same scholar I once was, but as a version shaped by years of work focused on complexity, scale, and perspective. This evolution has deepened my inquiry and broadened the scope of questions I find compelling.

Also, I am gratified by the reception this work has received within the academic community. My recent writings have found interest in traditional scholarly venues but also in interdisciplinary forums. Colleagues have also expressed interest in how my experience can inform them and their institutional practices. As a result, I have been invited to contribute to panels and deliver speeches on leadership, governance, labor relations, as well as AI ethics and its impact on education.

Despite the interruptions caused by two decades of senior academic administrative leadership, I have produced an extensive collection of scholarly work documented in various forms of peer-reviewed publications.

~

My academic career—seventeen years as a lecturer, professor, and college-level administrator followed by two decades of senior leadership and then returning to active teaching and research—has reshaped my understanding of what it means to be a scholar. Traditionally, the roles of scholar and administrator are often seen as distinct, even oppositional: one immersed in intellectual inquiry, the other preoccupied with institutional management. Yet my experience has taught me that these roles cannot only coexist but also enrich one another in meaningful ways.

Even though leadership is intellectual work too, there were times during my administrative career when I certainly felt the loss of my scholarly identity. The metrics of success shifted: scholarly writings gave way to policies and citations to strategic outcomes. What I have come to understand is that scholarship is not only an activity but also a disposition—a way of perceiving, questioning, and engaging with the world. This scholarly disposition remained intact throughout my years in leadership; only its expression changed. It revealed itself in how I approached problems, synthesized information, and formulated initiatives. I now see myself not simply as a scholar who served in leadership, but as someone whose scholarship has been transformed by that service.

The questions I now pursue are informed by context and consequence, dimensions that were highlighted by administrative experience. My sense of audience has expanded beyond disciplinary peers, to include leaders, policymakers, and educators asking the same questions. Serving in administration and then returning to the faculty has created a dual identity for me. Scholarly identity need not be something we leave behind when we lead nor something we resume unchanged when we return. Rather, it can be something we retain and resume but also adapt and renew in a form shaped by time and experience.

My new scholarly identity has indeed been adapted and renewed to include interest I thought was not possible in my earlier research career. I talked earlier about my interest in history and the fact that I was always intensely drawn to such topics, once considering pursuing a career as a historian. Yet it was my mother, with her wisdom and foresight, who guided me toward science and technology instead. As I have shared throughout this book, this path led to a rewarding and successful career for which I am truly grateful. Now, in this special phase of my career, I have returned to history and policy as a scholarly pursuit, and it has been fulfilling. This is consistent with my longstaging and ongoing advocacy through the Lebanese Information Center in Washington DC and at the United Nations on behalf of Lebanon's freedom and sovereignty. It is also building on my earlier work in advancing these causes that I began when I was still in Lebanon. I have already had the opportunity to give history lectures to communities that share my interest in such topics. I have even written the scholarly book mentioned earlier—*The Enduring Presence of Christianity in Lebanon*. The book explores how Christianity survived centuries of adversity in Lebanon and offers a roadmap for reform toward a new national identity for a peaceful and prosperous future.

I had the honor to serve as emcee for events organized by the Lebanese Information Center on Capitol Hill in commemoration of the anniversaries of the Lebanese Cedar Revolution and the withdrawal of the Syrian Army from Lebanon.

Taking the best of both worlds, history and technology, to an even higher level, Maura and I have also written a technical book on a computing subject of interest to both of us, *From Code to Cloud—Developing Web Applications*, which we have dedicated to the memory of our friend and mentor Jim McHugh.

Scholar-administrators who return to research are frequently perceived as exceptions or anomalies, when in fact they embody a continuum of academic identity that is increasingly relevant. As higher education grapples with demands for innovation, efficiency, and societal relevance, there is much to be gained from faculty whose scholarship is informed by leadership, and from leaders whose decision-making is grounded in scholarly rigor.

~

In my role as provost and senior executive vice president, my authority carried broad institutional influence, beyond just academic oversight. For me, my most important responsibilities were those that impacted people. Given my longevity at the university, from my time as an undergraduate student to the peak of administration, I got to know and develop close relationships with colleagues in all areas of the university and at all levels. My working relationships with others, whether they were vice presidents or groundskeepers, never changed because of a new title I received. I continued to greet individuals by name regardless of where they fell on the organizational structure. Above all, I had a particularly close relationship with our faculty, especially junior faculty. In fact, I was able to call every faculty member at our university by name.

As provost, and earlier as dean, I was privileged to oversee the recruitment and hiring of a large number of faculty for our university. At the conclusion of my service as provost, a majority of the NJIT faculty had appointment letters bearing my signature. Mentoring junior faculty is an institutional responsibility but also was, and still is, a personal commitment of mine.

In my role as dean, such mentorship involved creating a culture within the college that actively supported faculty development, fostered collaboration, and ensured clear pathways for success. While direct, day-to-day mentoring occurred at the departmental level, I set the tone by establishing strong mentoring frameworks, supporting fair and clear evaluation processes, and making access to resources for research, teaching, and service transparent. Through regular personal engagement that I was keen on maintaining, whether via collective or individual conversations, I was able to offer guidance on balancing academic responsibilities and thinking strategically about career trajectories, including leadership pathways, as well as opportunities to recognize faculty achievements.

In my role as provost, my mentoring work evolved to a broader, systemic level that enabled both individual success and university recognition. Mentoring in this context meant advocating for university-wide policies, systems, and culture that promoted faculty success. Doing so sent a clear signal that faculty, especially those at the early stages of their careers, were at the center of the academic community. This included explicit initiatives that provided access to professional development opportunities, support in navigating the broader university landscape, connecting faculty with funding opportunities and key resources, directing them to high-impact service roles that could elevate their profiles, and ensuring equitable workloads. Despite the intensity of scale and volume, I was able to continue engaging with individual faculty members by remaining visible and accessible through formal and informal meetings, events, and strategic communication.

Now, as a senior faculty member, my commitment to mentoring many of the junior colleagues who were hired by me and continue to seek my counsel and guidance remains at the forefront of my agenda, though in different forms. I have earmarked significant chunks of my time on campus to maintain open lines of communication with faculty, allowing me to understand their individual goals, strengths, and challenges, and to offer relevant advice on teaching, research, engagement, and career development. My approachability and ability to build a relationship of trust with the faculty have enabled me to provide constructive feedback and share my institutional knowledge in an environment of mutual respect, active listening, and a genuine interest in their growth and success.

PART THREE

Reflections

The Deek family on Christmas Eve 2025.

CHAPTER 7

A Life Interwoven

Over the course of my academic career, I have been fortunate to receive numerous honors recognizing my excellence in teaching, including several institutional awards and the designation of master teacher. These acknowledgments are meaningful to me not simply as milestones but as affirmations of a professional philosophy rooted in care, curiosity, and mentorship. Teaching, at its best, is an act of sharing. It is about shaping understanding, fostering growth, and believing in the potential of others. These same principles have guided me not only in the classroom but also at home.

As a father, I have always seen parenting as an extension of teaching, an even more intimate and lasting form of mentorship. My children, now accomplished in their own fields, are the living proof of this commitment. Raising them has been among the most rewarding endeavors of my life. At no point did I consider professional success to be a substitute for, or excuse from, being fully present in that role. More importantly, this journey has never been mine alone. Maura, herself a dedicated and exceptional teacher, has been my partner in every sense. Together, we built a life around shared values: a belief in knowledge as a force for good, a sincere commitment to our students and community, and, above all, an unwavering dedication to our family.

Her role as mother, educator, and confidante has been vital to everything we have achieved together. We both believe strongly that the lives we touch, whether in lecture halls or around the dinner table, are the truest measure of our legacy. We are grateful for the opportunity to serve as both teachers and parents in the fullest sense.

As we are on the subject of children and teaching, I want to share my thoughts about some words of writer, poet, and visual artist Khalil Gibran in his timeless work, *The Prophet*. It is a book I first read at a younger age but only truly understood as an adult, early in my teaching career. In this book, Gibran essentially shares his deep wisdom on the human experience: love, marriage, children, family, work, joy, sorrow, freedom, death, and more. I had read a version of this book that was translated from English to Arabic in Lebanon, as a requirement for a high school literature course, before I came to the United States. Soon after I arrived here, I bought it again in English, the language it was originally written in, but it sat on my shelf until I became a father for the first time. It was then that I felt compelled to revisit the poetic words he wrote about children, not because I remembered reading them before but because I had been listening to these prayer-like words, sung by Fairuz, the famed Lebanese artist, on a cassette I brought with me from Lebanon. Here are his words:

> Your children are not your children.
> They are the sons and daughters of Life's longing for itself.
> They come through you but not from you,
> And though they are with you yet they belong not to you.

There is not much I can add to these words, but that is not the only point of my bringing it up here. It is about something else. Captivated by the beauty of Gibran's words, I ended up reading the whole book again. Anyone who has read it will recognize its compelling nature. What resonated with me this time though were his words about teaching, which I had not noticed before. Gibran offered these profound insights into the nature of teaching and wisdom:

> The teacher who walks in the shadow of the temple, among his followers, gives not of his wisdom but rather of his faith and his lovingness…If he is indeed wise he does not bid you enter the house of his wisdom, but rather leads you to the threshold of your own mind.

Still relatively new to the profession, I was intrigued. The metaphor of a teacher walking "in the shadow of the temple, among his followers" struck me as a compelling call to reconsider my role as a teacher and the essence of true wisdom. The suggestion that a teacher's greatest gift is not the imparting of knowledge but the nurturing of faith, love, and self-discovery challenged my conventional view of teaching as simply the transmission of information or expertise, as I had understood and practiced it.

The statement about a teacher who "gives not of his wisdom but rather of his faith and his lovingness" emphasizes the intangible qualities that teachers bring to their students. Faith, in this context, is not religious dogma but a belief in the potential and inherent worth of each individual. A true teacher instills confidence in the students, encouraging them to trust in their own abilities and approach to their own knowledge construction. Also, love, in this context, is not about emotional bonds between people but an intellectual connection that at its foundation is a different type of relationship—a compassionate, selfless care that creates a space for development and maturity. By giving of their faith and lovingness, teachers become attendants rather than authority, fostering an environment where students feel trusted and empowered to find their own way.

The second part of Gibran's passage made his idea crystal clear: "If he is indeed wise he does not bid you enter the house of his wisdom, but rather leads you to the threshold of your own mind." The distinction between mere instruction and true wisdom could not be more obvious. Wise teachers do not seek to impose their own beliefs or knowledge onto their students. Instead, they act as catalysts, helping students realize their own truths and uncover their own insights. The "house of wisdom" symbolizes the teacher's own understanding and wisdom, which, while valuable, is not the ultimate destination for the student. The "threshold of your own mind" represents the beginning of the student's personal journey of discovery and the limitless possibilities for knowledge acquisition. A wise teacher recognizes that true learning is not about memorizing facts or adopting another's perspective but about awakening one's own curiosity, critical thinking, and inner wisdom.

The metaphor of the temple further enriches Gibran's message—in worth, depth, and impact. The temple, a revered space often associated with divine rituals, sacred knowledge, and spiritual enlightenment, frames the role of a teacher within a larger, humbling context. By walking "in the shadow of the temple," the teacher remains humble, acknowledging that wisdom is not something they possess exclusively but something that is accessible everywhere and is there to be acquired. The shadow suggests a presence that is felt but not seen, much like the subtle influence of a great teacher. The teacher's role is not to dominate or overshadow but to gently guide, allowing students to find their own path to enlightenment.

Humility and respect in the teacher-student relationship are at the core of education. While this is not always the case, it is essential to assert and embody these principles. By doing so, we challenge the traditional hierarchy, where the teacher is the sole source of knowledge, and the student is a passive recipient. Instead, we promote a dynamic, reciprocal relationship where the teacher's primary role is to inspire and facilitate self-discovery. This approach aligns with my educational philosophy that emphasizes critical thinking, creativity, and personal discovery over rote learning.

This is the essence of knowledge sharing: the greatest teachers are not those who simply dispense information but those who inspire faith, love, and self-discovery. We must not seek to fill the minds of our students with our own wisdom but to kindle the curiosity and critical thinking that lies within each one of them. In doing so, we guide the students not toward our house of wisdom but to the threshold of their own, where the true journey of learning begins.

Education, at its best, is not about control or conformity but about liberation and the celebration of individual potential. It also resonates with the idea that true wisdom is not something that can be handed down like a textbook. It is a deeply personal and evolving understanding that individuals must cultivate for themselves. While a teacher's faith and lovingness create the conditions for this growth, the journey itself belongs to the student. By leading students to the "threshold of their own mind," we help them recognize their potential and commit to a lifetime of learning.

Not only did the metaphor of a teacher walking "in the shadow of the temple, among his followers" compel me to reconsider my teaching style, but it also brought back memories of the national assessment approaches to which the Lebanese students were, and to a large extent still are, subjected.

Important test results can alter academic paths, influence long-term career trajectories, and change lives. As is the case in Lebanon, some high-stakes exams are designed to act as gatekeepers and to provide opportunities to those who the exam reveals are best able to benefit: fewer university spots than applicants, some believe, requires a filtering mechanism. However, assessment centered on memorization of facts or test-taking strategies—both the result of standardization that fuels gatekeeper exams—rather than deeper understanding do not lead learners to the threshold of their own mind. Moreover, a single exam cannot fully account for a student's abilities or potential. And the intense pressure faced by students that causes them stress and anxiety, sometimes lasting for many years, remains a concern for any educator.

Instead of one decisive exam, students should be graded over time and by multiple measures that encourage consistent effort. A portfolio of work compiled during an academic year including exams, essays, research projects, presentations, and other representative outputs of students' work shows depth of understanding, mastery of content, problem-solving skills, and communication abilities. It can be argued that this continuous assessment is harder to standardize, time-intensive to implement, and challenging to scale. It also requires strong safeguards to keep grading fair across schools.

While high-stakes exams are simple, scalable, and impartial, they are stressful. In contrast, the alternatives are more complex, less consistent, but more fair to the diverse applicants who want to find their place in post-secondary education. Supporting student learning, not standardized testing, should be the aim of assessment. No single measure can define a student's future. No single measure should limit the opportunity to learn.

~

I have taken Gibran's wisdom a step further in my own practice. I believe that the acquisition of knowledge can be effortless if we make sure it is abundant and freely accessible. Unlike any other asset, knowledge is the only commodity that appreciates in value only when it is freely shared. However, in the world of assets, we are often taught to accumulate wealth, collect valuable items, and invest in commodities or property. These physical assets typically appreciate, but sometimes hold, or even lose, their value over time based on market conditions, supply, and demand. Knowledge, though, is fundamentally different. It does not respond to scarcity or possession in the same way as traditional markets do because its true value emerges not through hoarding but through sharing. This concept speaks to the power of knowledge and the potential collective benefit for humanity from generous collaboration.

Knowledge, by its very nature, is limitless. Unlike tangible goods, which exist in limited quantities and are subject to wear and depletion, knowledge is an intangible asset that can expand evermore. The more knowledge is shared, the more it has the potential to grow and cause benefit. When we impart what we know, we do not lose anything; rather, we multiply its value. This is one of the most profound aspects of knowledge; it is not diminished by being shared, but enhanced. As a computer scientist, like many others in my field, but more so as an educator, I feel that I am in a unique position to advocate for and defend the principles of open and accessible software. In 2007, I published, with Jim McHugh, the book *Open-Source: Technology and Policy* (Cambridge University Press). We offered an in-depth assessment of the past and present, and envisioned the potential future for free and open-source software—challenging an influential software industry entrenched in its closed, proprietary models. The open-source movement is now fundamental to science and technology, and its influence continues to expand. The work of open-source advocates has democratized access to knowledge and resources, creating a more even field for people to participate meaningfully in education and the professions.

When knowledge is disseminated, it is allowed to evolve and spawn new ideas. When one person shares their understanding or insights, it does not simply transfer to others; it can spark new thoughts, innovations, or applications. The more people are involved in the exchange of ideas, the more possibilities are created, and the value of the knowledge expands. I see this as analogous to scientists who share their findings with the scientific community in the form of publications and presentations, contributing to further research and breakthroughs. Similarly, the teachers who guide students in their knowledge acquisition help create future cadres of learned people, leaders, and thinkers. In both cases, the knowledge shared creates a ripple effect that grows and impacts many, thereby appreciating in value.

This is particularly evident in the realms of science, technology, and society. Think of the world's greatest thinkers—Plato, Einstein, Curie, or contemporary figures like Stephen Hawking, Richard Dawkins, or Bill Gates. While some profited, and rightly so, these individuals did not just accumulate knowledge for their own benefit; they shared it, sometimes at great personal or professional risk, and in doing so, they sparked movements, revolutions, and entire industries that benefited countless future generations of people besides themselves. This cycle continues when individuals who receive that knowledge contribute to it in new ways; the value of the original idea increases over time. Such cumulative gain does not occur with money, real property, or any other asset. Unlike physical possessions, knowledge does not need to be stored or guarded since it flourishes when it is given away and placed in the open domain. This is precisely what I advocated for—Open Sourcing Knowledge—in the development of CSLA's second strategic plan, which I led, along with Norbert Elliot, in 2009.

~

One of the unique qualities of knowledge is that treating it as an egocentric asset offers no real advantage to its hoarder. While it is certainly possible to hold on to knowledge for personal gain, the true power of knowledge is realized when it is shared for the collective good. Whether it is in education, public health, or technology, the act of sharing knowledge has the potential to positively impact individuals, entire communities, nations, and even the world. The dissemination of medical knowledge during the recent global health crisis provides vivid evidence that knowledge sharing is more crucial than ever. The rapid sharing of research results, data, and resources was essential in developing vaccines, understanding transmission, and implementing preventative measures. This global knowledge sharing and collaboration helped safeguard an untold number of lives, underscoring the profound impact that knowledge can have when shared without reservation.

We can contribute to this collective benefit by offering our expertise and experiences to others—whether through formal teaching, sharing educational resources, mentoring a colleague, or helping someone solve a problem. We have the power to elevate others by sharing the knowledge we have gained. In doing so, we not only increase the value of that knowledge but also foster a culture of good will, mutual benefit, and trust.

While knowledge appreciates in value when shared, the opposite happens when it is hoarded. Hoarding knowledge often reflects insecurity or a lack of trust in others. The belief that keeping information hidden gives us an advantage is misguided. In fact, those who actively share their knowledge often find that it leads to greater recognition, respect, and success. It is through the exchange of ideas that we solve problems, break new ground, and create positive change in the world. The more it is shared, the more valuable knowledge becomes, not just to ourselves but to society as a whole.

~

The path we travel is seldom straightforward. We make plans, set goals, and take action, but the journey can be filled with setbacks, failures, and moments of doubt. Yet these very obstacles often emerge as vital experiences that shape us into the people we want to be. The detours, missteps, and challenges might feel frustrating in the moment, but they often lead to better outcomes than we could have imagined. My own life experiences affirm this. While I cannot guarantee the same for everyone, to reassure and prod my children to hold onto hope when they are agonizing over personal or professional matters, I often tell them: "… in the end, everything will fall into place exactly the way you want it to."

This is one of my own favorite sayings. It took me time to appreciate this for myself, but as soon as I accepted this belief, I began to convey these sentiments to my children and others. I have already spoken about how life, for me, has been a journey marked by unexpected shifts and moments of surprise. At times, it felt chaotic and unpredictable, leaving me wondering if everything would ever unfold as I had envisioned. Looking back, I can identify moments when I was unsure, frustrated, or uncertain about the future. Yet with time, things steadily came together, forming a clearer picture over time, sometimes in ways I could not have planned or expected.

This was especially true when I first arrived in the United States. Without sufficient command of the language, I quickly enrolled in a highly technical and challenging discipline, graduated, found employment, and advanced through the ranks beyond what I thought achievable. There were other challenging times as well, including when I was completing my PhD while holding a demanding full-time teaching and administrative position, teaching at two additional colleges as an adjunct, and raising three children with Maura. I questioned whether I would have the mental and physical stamina to do all this.

Yet I learned there is a certain wisdom in having faith in the journey and believing that, "in the end, everything will fall into place exactly the way you want it to." This belief reflects an essential truth: life, in its own unique way, often unfolds according to a greater plan, one that aligns with our desires and aspirations, even when the road ahead seems unclear. Trust and confidence will help too.

In a world that values instant gratification, the idea that things will come together in due course might sound overly idealistic or unrealistic. However, the key to this belief is trust. Trust is not about waiting for things to happen by themselves; it is about having confidence that effort and time will eventually lead to the right outcome. Many times, I became anxious and restless, wondering whether things would actually fall into place, or wanting success to happen quickly, but I learned that genuine advancement is a gradual process. The confidence to trust that things will work out does not come from a passive attitude, but from an understanding that consistent effort, learning from experience, and giving ourselves room to develop will lead us to the place we need to be.

In retrospect, I see how each experience, no matter how difficult, was a piece of the complete mosaic—helping me to refine my goals, teaching me valuable lessons, and ultimately guiding me toward a path that fit best. A career setback, for example, that initially seemed like a failure, later led to new opportunities, meaningful learning, personal development, and greater self-understanding. These challenges, in essence, are not roadblocks but detours that often lead to a more genuine and rewarding path than what we initially anticipated. They force us to be resilient, to innovate, and to grow in ways we otherwise would not.

~

"Everything will fall into place exactly the way you want it to" does not mean that life is a sequence of random events. Nor is it about blind optimism or waiting for fate to intervene. Rather, it is about aligning our values and our efforts, allowing the process to unfold both intentionally and naturally. The importance of congruence between intentions and actions is emphasized when we know what we want and how we will achieve it. The more we focus on these intentions and take deliberate actions toward our goals, the more we begin to consider opportunities that might have otherwise gone overlooked. These opportunities may not always be in the form we expect, but they can guide us forward toward our objectives, making it easier for things to eventually come together.

As a child, we often visited my maternal grandparents, who lived about three miles away from us. This allowed me to spend some time on my grandfather's farm helping him with his chores, like building a retaining wall or making an irrigation canal. Often, though, I just wandered around, drawn to the subtle wisdom nature offered. One sight in particular always captured my imagination— a fig tree or a flowering plant sprouting stubbornly from the side of a rocky cliff, clinging to life where there was barely any soil, no tending gardener, and little reason to grow.

I used to wonder how a seed got there in the first place; how anything could survive, much less flourish, in such a harsh place. But over time, I came to realize that such a sight is a symbol: a living embodiment of intentions and determined resilience. That tree or plant did not have the luxury of rich soil, generous rains, or constant sunlight. It had only a crack in the rock, and a will to grow. Still, it pushed through. Still, it stood. It did not just survive; it made something beautiful out of the impossible.

In the example of a plant struggling to survive in a harsh environment, I believe there is a powerful truth for us. Life is not always a nurturing environment. Often, we find ourselves in hard places, uncertain places, where it seems nothing good could ever flourish. But just like that plant, with intention, we can rise through the cracks. With perseverance, even the smallest seed of hope, of courage, of knowledge, we can break through stone and bloom. Change takes time to unfold. But in time, with a strong will and persistence, something beautiful will sprout.

Trusting that everything will come together involves having confidence in the process, even when it is difficult to understand why things are happening the way they are. The compelling argument for trust is that it allows us to release the need for control and accept unfolding events without constant worry or fear. This requires a shift in mindset, from one of anxiety and uncertainty to one of confidence and open-mindedness. It is about acknowledging that sometimes the flow of nature works in ways we do not fully understand. What might seem like a setback now can be the exact experience needed to propel us forward. If we manage to accept this premise, we can develop the trust that events will unfold as they should.

This belief does not imply that I should be passive and let events unfold. I continued to act, pursue my goals, and work to create the outcomes I desired. But it taught me to balance effort with confidence, both of which are necessary in bringing us closer to our desired outcomes. Effort without confidence can lead to frustration, while confidence without effort can lead to stagnation.

Of course, many times things did not settle into place in ways that I expected, and coming to terms with that is part of the journey. If we are willing to accept both the challenges and rewards that come our way, and allow ourselves space for development, learning, and exploring different opportunities, we may still find that things have fallen in place in ways we never would have imagined or anticipated—but in ways we can embrace.

The life I built with Maura, Matthew, Andrew, and Rebecca, piece by piece, is proof of this even as the old one, my real first life in Lebanon, has never left me. Charles and Isabelle will, one day, bear witness to the truth of just how wonderfully everything, and everyone, eventually falls into place.

CHAPTER 8

Passionate Leadership

I am often asked questions about success and leadership and the qualities that a person must encompass to succeed and lead. While I am not an expert or a scholar on this subject matter, to answer these questions, I usually try to think about my experiences by reflecting on how I grew into my various academic and administrative roles. I share some of my thoughts on this here.

To start with, there are a number of factors that lead to success and contribute to the development of leaders, shown through tangible progress made. Passion is one of these important factors. But passion, on its own, lacks direction. It must be coupled with a focus on people and process. Only when these elements reinforce one another can we achieve something that is not only worthwhile but also successful.

Passion is one of the defining characteristics that has guided my personal and professional journey. It drives motivation, supports long-term goals, and plays a central role in turning ambition into concrete results. My own motivation started with passion. It shaped my decisions, my work ethics, and my approach to leadership. Reflecting on my journey, I realize that success has never been an end goal. Instead, it has always been the byproduct of a deeper process that included hard work, dedication, and staying grounded in what I believed was right, especially in hard moments. Leadership, too, was never something I actively pursued for its own sake. It developed gradually as a result of living my life deliberately and focusing on meaningful work, with intent and purpose.

When I walked into that classroom in 1985 to teach my very first class as a newly appointed teaching assistant, I was not thinking about eventually becoming provost of a university. I was not motivated by titles or accolades. Instead, I was driven by circumstance, curiosity, and genuine interest in learning through teaching. I gave my undivided attention to every task, every lesson, and every interaction, not because I expected recognition but because I found joy and fulfillment in the process. Passion kept me focused. It guided me through challenges, inspired me to work through discomfort to grow, and helped me find openings where others saw dead ends. Passion allowed me to persist when the way forward was unclear and others gave up.

Passion, however, is not just about enthusiasm or excitement. It is about the intent. It is about making decisions that reflect what matters most to you. For me, this meant embracing every role I took on—whether as a student, a teacher, or an administrator—with a sense of responsibility and a desire to make a positive impact. For example, I believed that if I approached my teaching with passion, I could inspire my students to approach their learning with the same passion. This belief has been at the core of my leadership philosophy. True leadership, I have learned, is not about authority or control; it is about influence, inspiration, and actions. It is about creating an environment where others feel empowered to cultivate their genuine interests and realize their utmost potential.

Throughout my career, I have seen how passion can spark engagement in others. When you are genuinely passionate about what you do, it resonates with others. It builds trust, fosters collaboration, and creates a sense of common goals. As a leader, I have always sought to model the way forward, demonstrating through my actions that commitment and perseverance are the bedrock of accomplishment. I have encouraged my children, nieces and nephews, students, colleagues, and friends to embrace their own passions, take measured risks, and transform hardships into moments of progress. By doing so, I have witnessed the transformative power of passion, not only in my own life but in the lives of those around me.

Of course, passion alone is not enough. It must be accompanied by discipline, resilience, and openness to growth. There have been moments in my journey when I faced setbacks, doubts, and failures. Yet it was my passion that kept me going, reminding me of why I started and what I hoped to achieve. It gave me the strength to adapt, to innovate, and to keep moving forward, even when the road was difficult. It taught me that success lies in the process, not merely the outcome.

Looking back, I appreciate the role that passion has played in my life. It has supported my accomplishments, sustained my hopes, and served as a basis for my leadership. It has allowed me to approach every challenge with optimism and every opportunity with gratitude. More importantly, it has enabled me to make a difference, not only in my own life but in the lives of others. When I resumed my academic journey, as a professor away from administration, I recommitted myself to living and leading with passion, understanding that this drives my growth and encourages others to find their own motivation. This is where it all started decades ago, and it is what continues to guide me now, every day. It connects my past, present, and future by reminding me that success and leadership are not defined by where you end up, but by how you choose to get there.

For me, passion is more than just a characteristic. It is a core philosophy. It is the belief that both what I do and how I do it matters, and that my efforts can create a lasting impact. It is a recognition that outcomes worth being proud of are born not just from results, but from the time and intention invested in their process.

And, most importantly, it is about choosing to put people I encounter on my journey first and foremost because the outcome is actually a reflection of the people as well as the process.

~

At the heart of every meaningful endeavor are the people involved. Throughout my life, I have prioritized relationships, recognizing that personal connections are essential for effective teamwork and results. My mother's wisdom, "Acknowledge each person according to his or her God-given abilities," has been a guiding principle. This simple yet profound statement underscores the importance of valuing individuals for their unique talents and perspectives.

I have always surrounded myself with smart, capable people, including those who challenge my thinking. A range of perspectives is essential for balanced thinking. When we engage with people who see the world differently, we are forced to question our assumptions, refine our ideas, and grow intellectually and emotionally. Disagreement, when approached with respect and openness, illuminates paths to solutions and enriched perspectives. I have learned that listening is just as important as speaking. When we listen with intention, we gain insights that we might otherwise miss.

No one is good at everything, and that is fine. I observed early on that some individuals excel in technology, while others have a gift for writing. Some are innovative thinkers, while others are intuitive problem-solvers. Recognizing and appreciating these differences allowed me to build teams that transform individual strengths into collective power. In this way, collaboration became not just a strategy but an ingrained practice. My mother's words remind me to recognize the strengths of others and to seek out those whose abilities complement my own.

Throughout my personal and professional life, I have seen the power of putting people first. Whether it was working on a team project, mentoring a colleague, or simply being present for a friend, the relationships I have nurtured have enriched my life and contributed to my success. People are not just a means to an end to help me achieve my goals; they shape the goals themselves. By valuing and supporting others, we create a foundation that can withstand challenges and foster achievements.

~

The process is a journey of learning, growing, and striving for excellence, even in the face of challenges. My approach to any task, no matter how trivial, has always been to give it my best effort. This is not because I seek reward or recognition, but because I believe that everything I undertake is a reflection of my own abilities and values.

Engaging fully in the process requires discipline and a willingness to have an open mind. It is not enough to, like a machine, execute tasks; we must engage fully, seeking to understand and improve at every step. My mother's saying, "Not everyone will take valuable advice; some people have one ear like a slanted roof and the other ear like a rain gutter," speaks to the importance of being attentive, receptive, and humble during the process. Humility is central to this understanding. I have always believed that I can learn a great deal from others, but only if I am prepared to listen, accept help, and remain open to ideas that differ from my own. This openness has brought me benefit and exposed me to perspectives and experiences I would not have been able to reach on my own.

One of the most challenging periods of my life was preparing for my PhD qualifying exams while balancing family and work responsibilities. I was married with two children and a third on the way, teaching at multiple colleges, and juggling countless other commitments. It was during this time that I truly understood how a process determines a desired outcome and, more importantly, the value people bring to both.

Maura became my partner in this journey. While I was at work, she would read my books, highlight key points, and annotate difficult concepts, creating study guides for me to use when I returned home in the evenings. Her support was invaluable, and it taught me that a meaningful process depends on collaboration, extending beyond individual effort. Collaboration strengthens perseverance and leads to an appreciation of each other's skills, experiences, and efforts. The process is also about resilience. There will be setbacks and moments of doubt, but it is through these challenges that we grow stronger if we stay focused and find meaning in the path to get there, rather than solely the endpoint. By embracing the process, we develop the skills and knowledge to accomplish our tasks but, just as importantly, the character needed to achieve our meaningful goals.

~

I learned that successful outcomes depend on collaboration and shared effort. The outcome is shaped by the harmony between people and the process behind it. It is the tangible result of our efforts and the lessons we have learned, but it is also a reflection of the relationships we have built, the impact we have made, and the experience we have lived. My mother's saying, "A well sourced by a spring will never drain," captures this idea perfectly. When we invest in each other and commit to a thoughtful, supportive process, the impact of the outcome is lasting.

In a professional context, it typically requires the contributions of many, each bringing their unique skills and perspectives to produce tangible value. This is why I have always prioritized teamwork and sought out individuals who challenge and inspire me. To me, the product has never been just an end result, despite its importance, but the relationships and the growth that emerges from the process.

Moreover, the product embodies the principles we believe in. When we emphasize people and process, the outcome becomes more than just a goal achieved—it becomes a symbol of collaboration, appreciation, and care. It is a reminder that the quality of success depends on both the outcome and the process. In every project, whether personal or professional, I have strived for outcomes that reflect the best of what people and process can achieve. By doing so, I recognized and respected those who had been part of my journey.

~

I shared the story of preparing for my PhD qualifying exam while juggling three jobs not to cite a personal accomplishment, but to highlight the intersection of people, process, and product. Central to this challenging period for me was a life partner who is also a computer scientist, Maura, whose steadfast support reshaped my understanding of success. Her role in creating study guides, annotating complex concepts, and highlighting key points while I was at work underscored the importance of teamwork in overcoming life's challenges. This also speaks to how shared efforts and mutual appreciation can elevate individual aspirations into collective achievements, which leads me to the three enduring lessons I learned in the process: collaboration, perseverance, and appreciation.

The first lesson is the significance of collaboration. Success is often portrayed as the result of individual brilliance, but my experience proved otherwise. Maura's active involvement in my academic journey demonstrated that collaboration can amplify one's efforts. Her presence made my workload manageable and enriched my learning. This revealed a fundamental reality: true achievement is rarely a solo endeavor. Success is often made possible by the contributions of others who believe in your goals and are willing to invest their time and energy to help you succeed.

The second lesson is the value of perseverance. Balancing three jobs while preparing for a PhD qualifying exam certainly required resilience and determination. However, Maura's perseverance stands out as equally remarkable. Her consistent efforts to support me reflected a commitment to our shared journey. Perseverance, I came to realize, is not just about enduring hardships but also about finding ways to advance relentlessly, even when the path is daunting. Maura's dedication is a reminder that perseverance is actually a collective effort, sustained by the encouragement and support of those who care about us.

The third lesson is the importance of appreciation. Expressing appreciation is a foundation for sustaining any successful partnership but also the motivating force behind the pursuit of shared goals. Such lessons taught me the importance of recognizing the contributions of others and their invaluable support, reminding me that success is often built on the sacrifices and efforts of those around us. Maura's faith in my abilities and commitment to our shared future motivated her to invest her time and expertise without expectation of a specific return. Her example reminds me that gratitude is an essential quality for the recognition of value, kindness, or positive experiences that strengthen relationships and foster a culture of mutual support. When appreciation is present, it enables both parties to contribute wholeheartedly.

Beyond these lessons, my journey highlights the profound impact of partnership and shared commitment. It also reminds me that success depends on both individual work and the collaborative efforts of those alongside us. By embracing these values, I was able to navigate life's complexities with resilience and achieve goals that might otherwise have seemed insurmountable. This reflects the core human drive, the bonds, and the love that make extraordinary achievements possible.

CHAPTER 9

Purposeful Leadership

Perhaps I did well in life because I was lucky. However, I cannot dismiss the decisions I made and the advice I received in making these decisions. My brothers pursued careers in civil engineering and architecture while my intention was to become a historian, not a scientist. When the time came to consider college, my mother dispensed her wisdom in her own subtle way. She did not try to dissuade or persuade me, but simply pointed out, "Your passion for history will endure, but the scientific discipline will open up for you paths one can only imagine." This advice has allowed me to have the best of both worlds.

My mother's words encapsulate a profound wisdom that transcends the immediate context of choosing a career path. They reflect a delicate balance between pursuing one's interests and considering opportunities beyond the familiar. The depth of this wisdom lies in encouraging individuals to pursue their interests while remaining open to unexpected possibilities. In other words, stay flexible.

Given my profession, I am often asked by college-age students and their parents for advice on what disciplines to choose or what career path to seek. Probably the most common advice I have shared is not on what to study or what profession to pursue but to simply stay flexible.

~

Passion may or may not be fleeting. It can be a temporary feeling, but it can also be a firmly rooted force that sustains and fulfills us. This depends on our personality, character, experiences, and more. For me, history was more than a subject; it was a lens through which I understood the world. My mother's wise observation acknowledged the enduring nature of my interest, which could be nurtured regardless of the path chosen. It was an acknowledgement that our deepest interests are not easily extinguished by external circumstances. They remain a part of us, shaping our perspectives and gratifying our lives, even when they are not the primary focus of our professional endeavors.

However, my mother's wisdom extended beyond a mere reassurance. Despite her limited education, she asserted that a scientific discipline, or any unfamiliar field, can open doors to unimaginable opportunities. This is a subtle yet powerful encouragement to step outside one's comfort zone. While committing to our interests provides us with meaning, exploration broadens our perspectives. The scientific discipline, with its emphasis on logic, experimentation, and innovation, represents a realm of possibilities that may not be immediately understood or appreciated, especially at a young age. For me, it turned out to be exactly that. By embracing this discipline, I was able to access a world of opportunities that resulted in a fulfilling professional path and a stable future for my family.

~

Achieving the balance between passion and opportunity is a delicate lesson in adaptability and openness. In other words, flexibility, again. Too often, individuals feel pressured to choose between what they love and what seems prudent or promising. My mother's advice challenged this polarity, suggesting that the two are not mutually exclusive. Passion can coexist with pragmatism and pursuing one does not mean abandoning the other. In fact, reciprocity between the two can lead to a dynamic, more fulfilling life. In my case, this meant having the best of both worlds—a career in computer science that provided challenge and opportunity alongside a lifelong love of history that continues to satisfy my curiosity.

The wisdom of these words also lies in their recognition of life's unpredictable nature. While we may have unyielding interests and clear goals, life has its own path and often takes us in unpredicted directions. My mother's advice prepared me to embrace those uncertainties. By remaining open to new challenges and experiences, we equip ourselves to navigate the twists and turns of life with resilience and curiosity. This mindset fosters a sense of adventure, encouraging us to see every opportunity as a potential avenue for growth and discovery.

Moreover, my mother's approach to dispensing her wisdom is noteworthy. She did not impose her views or pressure me into a particular decision. Instead, she offered a gentle observation, allowing me to reflect and choose my own path. This subtlety reflects respect for autonomy and the importance of self-discovery. It is a reminder that wisdom is most effective when it empowers others to construct their own knowledge and make their own informed choices rather than dictating what those choices should be. Furthermore, the wisdom of these words lies in their ability to harmonize passion and opportunity, tradition and innovation, certainty and exploration. They remind us that our interests, enduring or not, need not limit us. By remaining open to the unknown, we can create a life that is both meaningful and full of anticipation. My mother's advice is not just a guide for choosing a career; it is a philosophy for living, a call to explore our lasting interests while daring to imagine and pursue the paths that lie beyond. Only by doing so, can we truly have the best of both worlds.

~

I have already talked about passion extensively and its role in pursuing my personal and professional choices. Purpose is just as important, in both realms. It is not just about grand gestures or lofty goals but about the everyday decisions we make, the values we uphold, and the impact we have on those around us. It means acting and speaking with intention, striving for progress over perfection, and balancing pride with humility.

I committed to living with purpose, despite challenges, because of the principles that have guided me along the way. In doing so, I learned that I could lead a life of meaning and impact that exemplifies who I strive to be and how I want to live my life. It is the thread that weaves through my decisions, interactions, and actions, giving them consequence and direction.

~

From a young age, I understood that purpose is not just about what you do, but how and why you do it. My mother often reminded me of the power of intentionality with a phrase I carry with me to this day: "Sometimes, a thousand words are not even worth one word; other times, one word is worth a thousand words." This simple, yet profound, statement has stayed with me throughout my life, shaping my approach to communication, leadership, and personal growth. I have always strived to act and speak with purpose, ensuring that my contributions are thoughtful, meaningful, and aligned with my values.

Looking back on my journey, I see how three fundamental traits have shaped who I am and given meaning to my purpose: principles, practicality, and patience. They have served as a compass through challenges, helping me to navigate complex decisions and build meaningful relationships. More importantly, they have given me a clear understanding of what matters most in life, offering inner satisfaction and motivation during difficult times.

~

Principles have consistently guided my actions, with integrity standing as the cornerstone of both my personal and professional life. I have always believed that success achieved without integrity is not true success. My mother often emphasized this value, using vivid imagery to drive home its importance. She would say, "Integrity is like a pane of glass; should it shatter, it will be impossible to bring it back to its flawless state." This metaphor has stayed with me, serving as a constant reminder of the fragility and irreplaceable nature of one's moral compass.

In a world where shortcuts and compromises are often tempting, and in many ways have become a norm, I have chosen to work by the rules, even when it meant taking the longer or harder path. This commitment to integrity has not always been easy, but it has always been worth it. It has earned me the trust and respect of colleagues, peers, and students, and it has allowed me to sleep soundly at night, knowing that I remained true to my principles. Integrity is not just a value I uphold; it is a legacy I hope to leave behind for my children and grandchildren, a testament to the idea that how one achieves something matters just as much as the achievement itself.

~

I believe that practicality is more important than perfection because perfection, in its truest sense, does not exist. This realization has been both liberating and empowering. Early in my career, I struggled with the desire to achieve perfection, spending countless hours refining projects, second-guessing my decisions, and fearing failure. Over time, I came to understand that this pursuit of perfection was not only unrealistic but also counterproductive. It delayed progress and overshadowed the value of what was already accomplished.

My mother, with her characteristic wit and wisdom, would often say, "One is without fault only if brainless." This humorous yet insightful remark reminded me that mistakes are an inevitable part of being human. Instead of striving for an unattainable ideal, I learned to focus on continuous improvement, doing the best I could with the resources and knowledge I had at the time. I learned that good is often enough, and that progress, no matter how incremental, is something to be proud of. By letting go of perfection, I welcomed risk, opened the door to growth, and allowed myself to learn in ways that I never could have if I remained paralyzed by the fear of making mistakes.

~

Patience is a virtue I have been fortunate to develop over the course of my life. It has become a cornerstone of my personal philosophy and a critical component of my approach to leadership. Patience is not merely the ability to wait; it is the capacity to maintain composure, compassion, and clarity in the face of challenges, setbacks, and uncertainty. It embodies the understanding that success and meaningful relationships take time to cultivate. As I reflect on my journey, I am reminded of the lessons I have learned about patience—lessons that continue to shape the way I lead, interact with others, and navigate the complexities of life.

To be a good leader, I have always reminded myself that patience is essential. Leadership is not about asserting dominance or rushing to conclusions; it is about guiding others with wisdom, empathy, and a steady hand. Patience allows a leader to listen attentively, understand different perspectives, and make decisions that are thoughtful and well-informed. It also helps to distinguish between confidence and arrogance, a distinction that is crucial for effective leadership. Confidence is rooted in self-assurance and a belief in one's abilities, while arrogance stems from a need to prove superiority. Patience enables a leader to embody confidence without crossing into arrogance, to lead with authority without alienating those they serve.

My mother once told me, "Assess and act according to each person or situation, as you cannot always behave reciprocally. If a dog bites you, would you bite it back?" This simple yet profound statement has stayed with me, reminding me that patience requires discernment. It is not about reacting impulsively or seeking revenge; rather, it is about responding thoughtfully and with intention. In leadership and in life, there will always be moments of conflict or misunderstanding, but patience allows us to navigate these moments with grace and integrity.

Patience also extends to how I treat myself. I am acutely aware that I am not perfect, that I make mistakes and fall short of my own expectations. But I have learned to be patient with myself and to forgive my missteps, as long as I learn from them. This self-compassion is not an excuse for complacency, but rather a recognition that growth is a process. It allows me to approach challenges with resilience and to view failures as opportunities for learning rather than reasons for self-doubt.

Patience is also at the heart of how I build and nurture meaningful relationships. It motivates me to give people the time and space they need to grow, to show their true selves, and to prove their worth. My mother often said, "You can welcome people based on their outward appearance, but you must see them off according to their words and deeds." This advice has taught me to be patient in my judgments, to look beyond first impressions, and to evaluate others based on their actions over time. It is a reminder that trust and respect are earned, not given, and that patience is essential in fostering genuine connections.

In leadership, this principle is particularly important. A leader must be willing to invest in people, providing opportunities to succeed and judging them fairly based on their efforts and contributions. Patience allows a leader to see the potential in others, even when it is not immediately apparent, and to guide them toward realizing that potential. It is through patience that a leader can build a team that is not only capable but also committed and cohesive.

Patience is more than just a virtue; it is a way of life. It is the foundation of effective leadership, the key to building meaningful relationships, and the source of strength in the face of adversity. Patience reminds us that success is not about speed but about perseverance, that growth is not about perfection but about progress, and that relationships are not about judgment but about understanding. Patience has been my compass, guiding me through the winding path of life and helping me to embrace its twists and turns with grace and resolve. It is a virtue I will continue to cherish and uphold, knowing that it is the key to a life of purpose, impact, and fulfillment.

Finally, patience has taught me that setbacks are not the end of the road but merely a detour. They are opportunities to learn, to grow, and to emerge stronger than before. By approaching challenges with patience, I have been able to turn obstacles into stepping stones and to keep moving forward, with resilience, even when the path ahead was uncertain.

~

By now, a number of logical questions may have arisen for anyone reading the previous chapter and this one, particularly regarding what leadership truly means and how one determines their own path as a leader.

Is it an innate trait, something you are born with? Is it something that can be taught and learned? Does it emerge naturally from the successes and failures of life? Is it forged in the fires of struggle and challenge?

I say the answer to these questions is "All of the above."

Leadership is a concept that has been studied, debated, and redefined across centuries, yet its essence remains elusive and deeply personal. The discourse on this topic is ongoing and will continue to be so. However, the experts' consensus is that leadership involves an innate quality but one that can be cultivated through experience and education. It emerges naturally from success and is shaped by adversity and hardship. This conversation lies at the heart of understanding what it means to be a leader.

Leadership is not a monolithic trait but a dynamic interplay of character, circumstance, and evolution. At its core, leadership can be defined as the ability to inspire, guide, forgive, and influence others toward a common goal. However, this definition only scratches the surface. True leadership transcends mere authority or management; it requires vision, empathy, and the capacity to connect with others on a human level. A leader is someone who not only charts the course but also empowers others to walk alongside them. In simple terms, it is both an art and a science, shaped by individual experiences and the challenges one faces.

Returning to the legitimate question of whether leadership qualities can be taught and learned: on one hand, we see leadership programs, workshops, and mentorship opportunities abound, suggesting that certain skills—such as clear communication, sound decision-making, and fair conflict resolution—can indeed be learned. These tools provide a foundation for effective leadership, equipping individuals with the techniques needed to navigate complex situations. On the other hand, leadership is more than just a set of skills; it is a mindset. While education can provide the framework, the ability to inspire and motivate others often stems from essential personal qualities like integrity, resilience, and emotional intelligence. These traits are not easily taught in a classroom but are often honed through lived experiences. This supports the idea that leadership emerges naturally from the successes and failures of life.

~

Success, in this context, is not merely the achievement of goals but the journey of development and self-discovery that accompanies it, reflected through the process and the people involved. Leaders often emerge in moments of triumph, where their ability to navigate challenges and seize opportunities becomes evident. Success can build confidence and credibility, two essential components of effective leadership. However, success alone does not define a leader; failures play an equally important role. What truly defines leadership is how one handles both success and failure. For success: whether with humility, gratitude, and the recognition of others. For failures: whether with a positive mindset, accepting responsibility, and analyzing what went wrong to learn from the experience. Too often, people prepare only for the outcome they desire. This inability to anticipate and plan for different possibilities, including those we do not want, leads to retreat and denial. True leadership lies in the ability to use any outcome, whether it be positive or negative, as fuel to move forward, stronger and wiser.

Furthermore, it is true that leadership is often forged in the fires of struggle and challenge. Adversity has a unique way of revealing character and testing one's resolve. Many of history's greatest leaders emerged from periods of immense hardship. Struggle teaches resilience, empathy, and the ability to persevere in the face of uncertainty. It forces individuals to confront their limitations, adapt to changing circumstances, and find creative solutions to complex problems. In this sense, leadership is not just about guiding others but about overcoming obstacles and emerging stronger on the other side. Challenge shapes leaders who are not only capable but also deeply compassionate and relatable.

Ultimately, leadership is a combination of nature and nurture, of success and struggle, of teaching and learning. It is not confined to a single definition or path. Some individuals may possess natural charisma and vision, while others develop their leadership abilities through deliberate effort and reflection. What defines all true leaders, however, is their unwavering commitment to a purpose greater than themselves. Whether in moments of triumph or defeat, leaders are defined by their ability to inspire, unite, and drive positive change.

Leadership is a multifaceted concept that defies simple categorization. It can be taught in part, but its essence often emerges from the convergence of personal qualities and life experiences. Success and failure both play crucial roles in shaping leaders, providing the context in which their abilities are tested and refined. Leadership, at its best, is a journey of continuous growth and a testament to the power of human potential. It is not just about leading others but about becoming the kind of person others choose to follow.

~

Leadership is not about proving you are the smartest. It is about creating the conditions where everyone can be their best, think freely, and succeed together. Intelligence, of course, plays a role in leadership, but it must be wielded as a tool rather than a weapon. Leadership is not about being the smartest person in the room or having all the answers. It is about using insight and clarity to mentor others, solve problems collaboratively, and create a space where everyone involved can grow and flourish. True leadership is marked not by how often we outthink others, but by how wisely we use our intellect to foster understanding, navigate complexity, and build trust.

When intelligence is used as a tool, it becomes a means of empowerment that helps people find their voice, their purpose, and their potential. But when intelligence is used as a weapon, it divides, creates fear, erodes confidence, and silences contributions. That kind of leadership might win in the short term but it does not inspire, and it certainly does not last. The best leaders I have known lead with both heart and mind. They understand that intelligence is most valuable when paired with humility and used in service of others, not at their expense. To be intelligent is not to be superior; it is to be responsible with our insights, mindful of our influence, and generous with our knowledge.

I have always believed that intelligence is not about outsmarting others but about solving problems through collaboration and creating opportunities for growth. My principles have allowed me to use my intelligence in ways that encourage rather than undermine, to approach challenges with curiosity rather than judgment. I recognize that there are people who are smarter than me, and others who may not be, and I am tolerant of both. Similarly, I understand that some individuals have supported me, while others subverted me, and I accept both. This acceptance reflects patience: a willingness to meet people where they are and to judge them based on their actions rather than my expectations.

~

Humility plays a crucial role in effective leadership. Far from being a weakness, it is a powerful leadership trait that fosters trust and openness, for both the leader and the team. Humility in leadership is not about being passive; it is about having the self-awareness to lead with confidence and fairness. It enables leaders to inspire, connect with others, and bring out the best in people. Perhaps the most challenging aspect of humility for me to internalize has been learning how to take pride in my accomplishments while remaining humble.

For much of my life, I struggled to accept praise or recognition. I would downplay my achievements, attributing them to luck or the efforts of others. While humility is a virtue that I faithfully aspired to, I came to realize that refusing to acknowledge my own contributions was not humility, it was a disservice to myself and to those who had supported me along the way. My mother had a humorous yet poignant way of addressing this. She would say, "He who is embarrassed in front of his wife will not have children." This playful remark, though it caused me some embarrassment, carried an honest truth: that self-effacement, when taken too far, can hinder recognition and satisfaction. It taught me that there is no shame in taking pride in one's accomplishments, as long as that pride does not turn into arrogance.

Over time, I learned that I can pursue excellence without losing empathy. I can be proud without being boastful. Real success is not just about how far I have come, but how sincerely I appreciate the path and the people who helped me walk it. Thus, I learned to accept praise gracefully, to celebrate my successes, and to share the credit with those who had contributed to them. At the same time, I remind myself not to let praise go to my head. I strive to maintain a balance between confidence and humility, recognizing that every achievement is the result of both individual accomplishment and collective effort. This balance has allowed me to stay grounded as I continue to seek excellence.

While it is important to strive for excellence, it is just as important to remain grateful throughout the journey. Accomplishments are meaningful—they reflect dedication, effort, and perseverance—but they alone do not define a well-lived life. Gratitude keeps us anchored. It reminds us that while our achievements matter, they are often made possible by a support system of family, teachers, colleagues, mentors, community—and by opportunities that not everyone has. Gratitude builds humility. It prevents entitlement because a grateful heart does not diminish ambition but fuels it with purpose and perspective. In this way, gratitude transforms success into something more meaningful, more human.

~

I have often reflected on forgiveness in both personal and professional contexts. I am not sure how much I can offer in this realm as the best way for me to describe my own state of mind, or reality, on this deeply personal topic is: a work-in-progress. But what I do know is that I am a person who does not hold grudges; I get over things easily. However, moving on is not the same as forgiving. For a long time, I thought of forgiveness as a superhuman trait, though I have come to realize it is not impossible. Perhaps it feels superhuman because it often involves letting go of intense emotions like anger, betrayal, or resentment—feelings that can be all-consuming.

Clearly, it requires a lot of emotional strength, vulnerability, and practice to overcome the hurt that makes forgiveness necessary in the first place. I understand why many people find it difficult to forgive, especially when they have been hurt purposefully, and that is totally understandable. I am one of those people. Understanding all of this has enabled me to make progress. I also realize reaching forgiveness, or starting on the road toward it, is often best achieved in stages.

First, forgiveness does not mean forgetting the wrongdoing we have been subjected to or ignoring our feelings. Rather, it is about choosing to release the grip that those negative emotions have on us, which can be a process that takes time and effort. I am beyond this stage.

Second, to believe and accept, one needs to experience the healing and inner peace that forgiveness can lead to. While it can feel, or be, incredibly difficult, it certainly is not something that requires superhuman powers—just a commitment to emotional maturity and a desire to move forward. I have experienced this.

Finally, while it can still seem superhuman at times, forgiveness is a very powerful human trait that can transform not only our relationships with others but also our own sense of peace. In fact, I have come to realize that forgiveness belongs in the same category as patience and humility. Based on my personal experience, it is something that we can work on and aspire to, like other desirable human qualities. This requires time.

One more word about forgiveness versus not holding grudges. Both are essential, but they involve different emotional processes and intentions. Forgiveness is a conscious decision to let go of resentment or anger toward someone who has wronged you. It involves acknowledging the hurt, processing the emotions related to it, and making a deliberate choice to release the desire for revenge or punishment.

Not holding grudges is more about not allowing past wrongs to continually affect your mindset or emotional well-being. It often implies that you are not dwelling on the offense and you have moved on from it without letting it have an ongoing impact on you. In short, forgiveness is a more intentional process of letting go of hurt, while not holding grudges is about not letting past offenses continue to affect your emotions or relationships. They often overlap, but they are not the same.

~

Although I never received formal education in leadership, I was fortunate to attain the highest leadership positions in my field. I cannot say for certain whether this was due to an innate ability, but I do know that, in general, I am highly observant and attentive to detail. I have always noticed the subtleties in people's behavior and organizational dynamics—things others might overlook—which allowed me to learn quietly, adapt promptly, and lead effectively by drawing insight from those around me.

Thus, I consciously wanted to learn from established leaders, and, throughout my career, I have focused on observing several key aspects of their leadership styles and management processes. I learned what should be done while leading by regularly noting and reflecting on the behaviors and decision-making approaches of others. I was able to integrate what I considered to be best practices into my own work style. More importantly, I learned what should not be done while leading by noting the behaviors and practices I should avoid such as those that can be detrimental to the success of individuals, teams, and the organization as a whole. By leading with empathy, integrity, transparency, and foresight and avoiding detrimental behaviors, leaders can build stronger relationships with their teams, foster trust, and lead with a greater sense of purpose and impact.

~

Let me start with what is "acceptable." In terms of decision-making, I made a point to understand the rationale behind the actions of established leaders by asking myself why they chose a certain path. This helped me grasp the logic and thought processes involved in their decisions. I also paid attention to how they handled consequences, especially when things did not go as planned. I observed whether they took ownership of the situation and how they pivoted to resolve issues that arose.

In terms of communication, I observed how leaders interacted with their team members, peers, and superiors. I took note of whether they used clear, concise language and how they tailored their messages to different audiences. I also closely watched how they handled difficult conversations, including managing conflicts or delivering tough feedback. I observed their ability to remain calm, listen actively, and ensure their points were understood. Additionally, I paid attention to their nonverbal communication, such as body language, tone of voice, and eye contact, all of which are crucial in assessing leadership qualities.

When it came to delegation, I observed how leaders assigned tasks and responsibilities. I noted whether they empowered others by giving them ownership of projects and how they ensured the workload was balanced. I also paid attention to their follow-up patterns and how they provided feedback and support without micromanaging.

Building relationships was another key area of focus. I watched how leaders built rapport with others—whether by showing genuine interest in people's lives, being approachable, or offering praise. I also noted how they handled diverse perspectives and managed teams with different personality types. It was important to see how they made everyone feel heard and valued. Additionally, I observed their approach to mentorship, paying attention to how they guided less experienced members of their teams and provided constructive feedback.

In terms of managing time and priorities, I observed how leaders prioritized tasks, especially when juggling multiple competing demands. I paid attention to whether they made quick decisions or took their time, and how they balanced short-term and long-term goals. I also watched their time-management strategies, noting how they set aside time for strategic thinking versus working reactively, and how they avoided distractions to stay focused on key objectives.

I closely observed how leaders approached challenges when solving problems, whether they remained calm under pressure and broke down complex problems into manageable steps. I also noticed how they encouraged creative solutions, whether they led with their own approach or involved the team in generating ideas. I paid attention to how they handled disagreements and differing opinions.

Finally, in terms of strategic thinking, I watched how leaders maintained a long-term vision, aligning day-to-day activities with larger organizational goals. I noted how they communicated this vision to others and steered the team toward it. Additionally, I paid attention to how they balanced tactical and strategic thinking, managing short-term tasks while keeping an eye on long-term objectives. These observations provided valuable insights into effective leadership practices.

~

Now, let me conclude with what is "not acceptable." Starting with micromanagement. I observed how it can undermine trust, stifle creativity, and create a demoralizing work environment. Leaders must avoided and reject the temptation to micromanage because it can prevent team members from growing and developing their own leadership skills. Effective leaders delegate effectively, trust their team, and focus on providing guidance and support rather than controlling every aspect of their work.

I noted that by being inconsistent—for example, frequently changing expectations or decisions without clear communication—leaders create confusion and frustration. Proactive leaders must maintain consistency in their actions and expectations, communicating any changes clearly to the team in order to help them remain on task and on time. Relatedly, when leaders avoid difficult conversations with their teams or team members, I observed how problems can fester and escalate, leading to persistent tensions and uncertainty, especially regarding performance. Difficult conversations need to be tackled head-on, providing timely, constructive feedback that offers direction and fosters success.

Playing favorites by giving special treatment based on personal biases is usually evident to team members and observers. It breeds resentment, divides teams, and can lead to a lack of motivation from others who feel undervalued. Fair leaders must strive to be honest and objective, treating all team members equitably. Similarly, shutting down new ideas discourages creativity and stifles innovation. Secure leaders foster a culture of open communication, encouraging ideas from all levels of the organization. Evading responsibility, on the other hand, damages credibility and trust, creating a culture of blame instead of accountability. Leaders earn more respect when they take responsibility for both successes and failures and demonstrate humility and integrity.

Being reactive instead of proactive leads to stress and poor decision-making, especially in tasks requiring firm deadlines or high-pressure situations. Relatedly, ignoring work-life balance of both team members and leaders can lead to burnout, reduced productivity, and dissatisfaction. Organized leaders anticipate timelines, challenges, and required resources, proactively managing obstacles before they escalate. They also promote a healthy balance between work and personal life.

Neglecting to recognize and appreciate team members' achievements is a leading cause of disengagement, decreased motivation, and high turnover. Failing to develop team members—whether through training, mentorship, or advancement opportunities—can also lead to alienation. Forward-thinking leaders invest in their team's well-being by providing growth opportunities and support to help them step into their own leadership roles. They also regularly acknowledge and celebrate the contributions of others.

~

In his poem *Ithaka*, Constantine Cavafy, a Greek poet born in 1863 in Alexandria when Egypt was under Ottoman rule, uses the metaphor of Odysseus's journey to suggest that the true value of life lies not in reaching a final goal, but in the experiences, knowledge, and personal growth gained along the way. The destination gives us a reason to begin, but it is the journey itself—shaped by curiosity, discovery, and patience—that gives life its meaning. Cavafy's words speak to me on a personal level, echoing the path my own life has taken. It is not the destination that it has shaped—it is the winding road, the moments of wonder, the people I encountered, the quiet trials, the gradual unfolding of understanding. In the journey itself, I have found meaning, purpose, and a sense of becoming.

As I begin to wind down a career that has given me more than I ever imagined, I do so with no regrets—only gratitude. Gratitude for the work, for the people, for the moments of challenge that refined me, and the moments of triumph that grounded me. This book is not a ledger of accomplishments, but an acknowledgment of a life that was made better by those who shaped me, believed in me, and stood with me. For all of it, I am deeply humbled and eternally grateful.

AFTERWORD

A Letter to Charles and Isabelle

Dear Charles and Isabelle,

I do not know when you will get to read this note from me to you. When this manuscript went to press, one of you was a little over a year old and the other was a month old. You may be too young to understand now, but one day, when you are older, I hope you will read these words and feel the love behind them. I may not be there to guide you in person, but my heart will always be with you as you grow, learn, and make your own way in the world. This letter is a small piece of my life, my thoughts, and the lessons I have learned along the way, shared with the hope that they may help you in your own journey.

Beside me, always, has been Maura, your grandmother, my partner in all things, with whom we built not just a life, but a home. Together, we raised a family of three children who now walk their own paths with empathy, integrity, and purpose. Two of them are your parents and the other is your aunt. Watching them step into their own personal and professional worlds as the cycle of life continues has been the greatest of all rewards, especially as we see them taking on the role of parents themselves.

If you are reading these words, I suspect that you have already gone through the earlier parts of the book. I wonder what you make of what I have written in these pages?

I have certainly experienced success in both my personal and professional life, but like most people, I have also faced my share of setbacks. There have been times when I hit a roadblock, when my plans were derailed, or when I was confronted with what felt like insurmountable obstacles. In those moments, values that range from faith to empathy, and much more in between, have been my greatest allies. They have allowed me to pause, to assess the situation, and to focus on the things within my control. Rather than lamenting what went wrong, I channeled my energy into finding solutions and continued on my journey. I will elaborate.

Keep the faith, no matter what comes your way.

Whatever my fears, I held onto a faith that grounded me, gave me courage, and reminded me that I was not alone in the journey. That trust helped me step forward, even when everything felt uncertain. While not overtly religious, as the son of a Melkite Greek Catholic father and Antiochene Syriac Maronite mother, I adhere to my Christian beliefs that I held as a child in Lebanon, where I was born. In fact, I have always identified as a person of faith and strived to uphold the core principles of my fundamental tenets. In navigating personal and professional challenges, I drew upon this foundation as a source of resilience. My faith provided a framework for confronting uncertainty and allowed me to manage fear with a sense of purpose and grounded perspective. My approach is to focus on the values and personal meaning behind my faith rather than the formal aspects of my religion. When I did share my values with my children and others whom I love or who may have been interested and receptive, I did so with respect for their freedom to choose their own values and form their own approaches in confronting challenges.

Whether you are pursuing your dreams, navigating difficult circumstances, or making significant life changes, fear can be an overwhelming emotion that can hold you back. It can keep you anchored in place and unsure of how, or whether, to proceed. We all face moments of fear and uncertainty, Charles and Isabelle, but to move forward you can counter fear with faith. This does not necessarily have to be faith in a specific religion or doctrine; it can be faith in yourselves, the process, and the possibility for positive outcomes.

"Do not be afraid" is one of the most repeated biblical phrases, offering comfort and reassurance in the face of uncertainty. You might not always understand why things unfold the way they do, but faith allows you to believe that there is meaning in your life and experiences. At the very least, it provides a way to face and navigate challenges with purpose. This belief in possibility counteracts fear by shifting your perspective from one of confusion to one of hope. Instead of focusing on what could go wrong, you begin to focus on what could go right.

Fear of the unknown, fear of rejection, and fear of failure are common forms of fear that might hold you back from realizing your potential. Fear is a natural and protective response to perceived danger or uncertainty that evolved as a survival mechanism, alerting us to threats. You fear what you cannot anticipate, what you do not understand, or what you believe might cause you harm. In these moments, your mind focuses on worst-case scenarios, and you become paralyzed by the idea that things might not go the way you want. However, the key to moving forward is recognizing that fear does not have to restrict or dictate your choices. Instead of letting fear control you, you can respond to it with logic: having faith in your ability to handle challenges, having faith in the process you employ to mitigate challenges, and having faith that things will unfold as they are meant to.

The belief that you are able to handle what comes your way, even when you do not yet have all the answers or tools, requires confidence. It also requires trust that you are capable of adapting and growing, even when you cannot see the end result. The lessons you will learn along the way, even the missteps, are learning opportunities. Faith will not necessarily eliminate fear, but it will give you the courage to act in spite of it. Courage enables you to look at fear as a signal rather than an obstacle that will stop you in your tracks. Fear is an indicator that you are on the verge of something that requires caution and contemplation.

Be patient, good things take time.

What I have learned from my experiences, dear Charles and Isabelle, is that success is rarely a straight line. It is a winding path, filled with twists, turns, and unexpected detours. Some people are fortunate enough to plan their lives and careers meticulously, but in my experience, they are exceptions to the rule. For most of us, success is a journey shaped by instinct, adaptability, and perseverance. I look back on my own life and career with a sense of wonder at where I am and how I got here. Much of my success has been the result of following my instincts and trusting my gut when the path ahead was unclear.

The wisdom of my mother, your great-grandmother, has been a source of comfort and guidance in these moments of uncertainty. She would often say to me and my brothers when we were young and struggling with a decision, "Whatever spot in the ocean you drink from, it will be salty." This metaphor has stayed with me, reminding me not to dwell on decisions; challenges and setbacks are an inevitable part of life. So, no matter where you find yourselves, there will always be difficulties to navigate. Patience allows you to accept this reality and to focus on what you can control. It enables you to move forward with resilience and determination until you realize satisfaction.

Patience also plays a crucial role in overcoming setbacks. In life, obstacles are inevitable, but you should maintain perspective when things do not go as expected. Instead of giving way to disappointment or discouragement, you can consider setbacks as temporary, knowing that you will find your way forward. With patience, you can assure yourselves that opportunities will still present themselves and that challenges are a normal part of the journey, not the end of it.

One of the most empowering aspects of patience is the confidence we place in ourselves. Moving forward requires that you are capable of learning, improving, and succeeding. Doubting your abilities, especially when you encounter significant difficulties, is normal, but recognizing that you are resilient and resourceful, and that you have, or can acquire, the knowledge and tools to face your challenges allows you to embrace uncertainty with confidence. This, in turn, encourages you to take calculated risks, knowing that even if you fail, you can learn from the experience and continue moving forward. This realization gives you the freedom to try new things, make mistakes, and grow into who you want to be. It is the foundation upon which courage is built.

By embracing trust in yourselves you can move beyond your fears and take meaningful actions. You can see the opportunities instead of the obstacles, you can view challenges as lessons rather than failures, and you can have the trust that you are capable of handling whatever comes your way. Your journey may not always be easy, but with patience as your guide, you can navigate it with confidence.

Honor your identity.

If you recall, the title of this book is *Portrait of an Expatriate: A Lebanese-American Story*, and that is the only place I used the word expatriate, but I also never defined it. The reason for this is because at the time I started writing the book, I was not certain of how I would like it defined because, in a way, I would be defining myself. Having completed the writing of this book, and as I write this letter to you, Charles and Isabelle, I feel that I now have a better understanding of myself and of the word expatriate, perhaps, even different from when I started.

Leaving my home country to complete my college education in the United States was the beginning of a major life shift. What started as a transitory period to study abroad has turned into a permanent settlement in a new country, where I built a career and created a family. Over time, this new place became home to me, and I adjusted to its language, culture, people, and way of life.

However, there is a complexity in this experience. While I have fully embraced my new homeland, I now feel different when I return to Lebanon, actually like an expatriate. The life I have built here is deeply rooted in me and, sometimes, the differences between my two worlds feel more pronounced. At the same time, Lebanon is still a part of me, and I carry it in my heart wherever I go. There are moments when I connect deeply to both sides, my original country and my adopted country. I now have been shaped by two cultures, two identities, and two homelands. I am comfortable with this duality, and I have come to realize that it is not about fully choosing one over the other, but about finding a way to merge them into who I am now. Indeed, the balance between the two comes naturally and, in a way, I have learned to exist as a blend of both. In this sense, I am both an expatriate and a native, simultaneously and equally belonging to two places.

While I have full confidence that you will grow up proud in this country, always remember the rich heritage that is part of you. Honor it, and let it remind you of the strength and resilience that runs through your veins. This balance of honoring your heritage and being proud of your nation is healthy and important, as long as you remain loyal to the country that gave you life and opportunities.

Focus on what you can control.

This mindset is a path to peace and progress. It took me time to truly understand the utility of this, but now that I do, I have often told my children, and many others, to worry only about the pieces they control because they can make them better. Dwelling on what you cannot control is a waste of energy.

It is easy to feel overwhelmed by life's constant flow of challenges, uncertainties, and the many things that lie outside of your control. Whether it is related to school, family, friends, work, society, global events, or even the actions of others, it may at times seem like there is much happening around you that is beyond your influence. However, I want to tell you as well, Charles and Isabelle, that you should focus only on the pieces you can control, because you do have the power to improve and alter those aspects of your lives. Stressing over what is beyond your reach is not only pointless but also a drain on your energy. Instead, take intentional actions to make tangible progress and direct your focus toward the things that you can change—your own actions and reactions. For example, focusing on learning new skills, enhancing your knowledge, or improving your emotional resilience allows you to take active steps toward improvement and growth in your personal and professional domains.

Focusing on what you can control requires coming to terms with the fact that your time, energy, means, and mental resources are limited. When you spend your efforts on things outside of your control—a range of possible scenarios and outcomes you cannot influence—you unintentionally make yourselves feel incapable, vulnerable, and defeated. These emotions often lead to stress and, potentially, anxiety, which can cloud and hinder your ability to move forward with the things you can influence. By concentrating on what you can control, you conserve and shift your energy toward things that you know that you can direct and improve.

The energy spent on worrying about what you cannot change is ultimately wasted. No amount of anguish or stress can alter the course of events that lie beyond your influence. By focusing on them, you lose sight of the range of actions you can take to improve your own situation, function optimally within your own environment, and contribute meaningfully to the wider world around you. This shift in focus begins with understanding what you can control. At the most fundamental level, you control your own minds and attitudes. Specifically, how you approach the problems you face, how you prioritize your time, and how you interact with others. By focusing on these things, you influence your actions in ways that enable you to make progress toward what is sufficient for your imperative to survive—and to thrive.

Seek to understand, not assume.

In a world driven by communication and exchange of ideas, understanding is essential for connection. Whether in education, professional settings, or personal relationships, comprehension is fundamental to navigating society's complexities. Yet, there is a nuanced distinction between not understanding something and misunderstanding it that we seldom pay attention to, and this distinction can have profound consequences. While not understanding something might be a temporary obstacle, to misunderstand is far more damaging because it distorts reality. In other words, to not understand is bad; to misunderstand is worse. Our increasingly digital society makes this even more complex.

Not understanding something is a natural part of life. Regardless of your intelligence and knowledge, you may encounter limits in what you comprehend at one point or another. Whether it is a difficult topic in school, a foreign language, a complex scientific theory, or a new concept in your profession, there will always be gaps in your knowledge. But this lack of understanding is not inherently harmful. In fact, it is a foundation to acquire more, or new, knowledge, a drive for curiosity and learning. Not understanding is an invitation to ask questions, seek clarification, and explore the subject further. It is a neutral state, one that holds the potential for growth. The only risk in not understanding something lies in the refusal to confront that ignorance, or worse, pretending that you do. If you fail to acknowledge your lack of understanding, you deprive yourselves of the opportunity to learn.

Misunderstanding, on the other hand, is far more perilous. When you misunderstand something, you are not simply un-informed; you are misinformed, often in a way that shapes your perceptions, decisions, and actions. Misunderstanding involves an incorrect or distorted interpretation, and this can lead to harmful consequences. For example, if you misunderstand a person's intentions, you might wrongly assume they are acting out of malice, which can lead to conflict and damaged relationships. Similarly, misunderstanding important facts in a professional setting can result in poor decisions, missed opportunities, or even failure. At its worst, misunderstanding prevents you from seeing others as complete individuals. It replaces your trust with suspicion and creates pathways for prejudice. If you allow misunderstanding to define your views of others, you sacrifice the understanding necessary for collective peace and progress in our world.

The problem with misunderstanding is that it often feels like understanding, even when it lacks depth or accuracy. If you believe that you know something when you do not, this false confidence can prevent you from revisiting your assumptions or seeking a deeper understanding. Misunderstandings often come from pre-conceived notions, biases, or incomplete information. As a result, they lead you to form conclusions based on false assumptions, and this distorted view of reality can influence not only your actions but also how you interact with the world around you.

There is humility in seeking clarity by first admitting when you do not understand something. Once you acknowledge your gaps in knowledge, you can take steps to clarify, investigate further, and ask the right questions. It is important to remember that there is nothing to be ashamed of in not knowing; only in failing to seek understanding. In both personal and professional relationships, it is essential to practice active listening and ask questions to ensure clarity. Taking the time to verify your understanding, especially when things seem vague or up to interpretation, can prevent the formation of misconceptions. It is far better to ask for clarification than to walk away with a misunderstanding that could later cause you, or others, harm. To misunderstand is to misrepresent reality, and that misrepresentation often leads to decisions based on faulty premises.

Embrace a modest mindset.

By cultivating a mindset that values modesty, we protect ourselves from the subtle dangers of an inflated ego. Ego, in its simplest form, is our sense of self. It drives our desire to succeed, be seen, and gain recognition for our efforts. It can be healthy or fragile. When our ego is healthy and balanced, it can provide pride and confidence. But when it expands unchecked, especially when it is fueled by unmoderated praise for achievements, or the like, it becomes destructive and provoking. When that happens, we risk disconnection from reality and reveal ourselves through arrogance, superiority, and entitlement. That is why I often tell my children that "something can go to your head only if there is room for it."

In reality, an inflated ego neither rises from strength nor conveys confidence, but instead it emerges from a gap in self-awareness, a space that is created when you lack emotional and intellectual maturity. This gap that you sometimes leave for your ego to fill often comes from a fragile or incomplete sense of self. If you base your worth solely on external validation, whether it is recognition from others, titles you are given, and accomplishments, real or per-ceived, you are setting yourselves up to be ruled by ego. A healthy ego is built on self-esteem and personal achievement. To lead and to grow, you must learn to manage that space with intention, mod-esty, and grace so your ego remains healthy.

A fragile ego, often rooted in deep insecurities, can also lead to narcissism. Narcissism emerges from an unrealistic self-image that craves constant external validation. Unlike those with a healthy ego, narcissists cannot handle criticism or failure without feeling personally threatened. Narcissistic behaviors can disrupt relationships, as individuals often seek validation rather than genuine connection. They may appear charming but lack emotional depth, leading to shallow interactions. Furthermore, their inability to accept criticism stunts personal growth, keeping them in a cycle of defensiveness and stagnation.

And so we return to the need for humility. The remedy to an unchecked ego is intellectual humility—the recognition that no matter how much you know or how far you have come, there is always more to learn and further to go. A truly wise person knows that their achievements or success are not the sum of who they are. When you approach life with this mindset, you recognize that your accomplishments, no matter how significant, are not collections of trophies to be displayed, but simply milestones on your journey of continuous learning. This way, instead of complacency, or settling for the satisfaction of past achievements, you are motivated to learn more, continue to grow, and help others along the way. This sense of awareness, Charles and Isabelle, will prevent the creation of a space in your heads where inflated egos can take root.

Remain flexible.

Taking responsibility means acknowledging that you are in control of the direction you take and the decisions you make. No single approach works for everyone when it comes to success, happiness, or fulfillment. What works for one person may not work for another, and that is also perfectly fine. While you cannot always control the world you live in, you determine your attitude toward it. When you take charge of your own story and trust in your abilities, you hold the power to create the lives that reflect your true selves.

The beauty of life lies in its boundless potential, and the freedom to shape it as you desire. What makes the difference is to remain flexible and believe in the process, including taking measured risks, exploring new paths, or challenging yourselves to grow in new ways. Along the way, you might make mistakes or face unexpected setbacks, but those experiences are fundamental to your growth. Each failure or misstep is simply an opportunity to refine your approach and learn what works best for you.

As you gain new experiences, you may discover new passions or interests. Your values may shift, or your priorities may change. Stay open to the process and trust that with each choice you make, you are creating a life that shines with its own distinct light. Whether you seek quiet contentment or bold adventure, true satisfaction comes from knowing that you have forged it to your will. At the heart of this perspective is the satisfaction that comes from knowing that your life is your greatest work, your personal legacy to craft as you see fit. Living life according to your own personal values is one of the most fulfilling choices you can make. Embrace the freedom to choose your path, balance your priorities, and craft the life you desire. Trust in your will and abilities and remember that you can make your life exactly what you want it to be.

Even in the face of challenges you will undoubtedly face, you can still be deliberate in how you respond. There are difficult situations that you will not be able to control, no matter how hard you try, such as natural disasters, but you can control your attitude toward them. Adopting a mindset of flexibility, perseverance, and gratitude can help you navigate obstacles. By concentrating on the things you can change—how you react to difficult situations or adversity, how you learn from your experiences, and how you interact with others—you can transform challenges into opportunities for your development.

Acceptance does not mean resignation; rather, it is acknowledging that the process of acceptance also helps reduce unnecessary stress. When you stop resisting what is beyond your control, you allow yourselves the composure to focus on what truly matters. You can move through life with greater peace and purpose, knowing that doing your best is the best you can do.

Your lives are shaped by those around you.

Life is an ongoing process of development and self-discovery, and one of the most significant ways we develop is through our interactions with others. People—whether family members, friends, colleagues, mentors, or even strangers—serve as mirrors reflecting our own behaviors, values, and choices. There is wisdom in observing and reflecting on the actions of those around us. We often assume that learning comes solely from those who guide us with explicit insights and exemplary actions. However, sometimes it is the flaws and failures of others that offer the most valuable lessons. Both positive and negative examples contribute to shaping who we become.

Every person you meet has the potential to teach you something valuable. You learn from all people, Charles and Isabelle. From most you learn what to do. From some you learn what not to do. While you are naturally drawn to learn from those who exemplify positive traits and behaviors, the mistakes of others also offer you important lessons about what to avoid. Life is not simply about imitating the successes of others; it is about discerning what works, understanding what does not, and using those insights to shape your own actions.

Throughout your lives, you will encounter individuals who inspire you through their principles, conduct, and actions. These are the people who set examples of integrity, kindness, diligence, and resilience; the qualities you admire and wish to emulate. When you observe someone behaving in a way that aligns with your values or demonstrates a desired outcome, you learn what is possible and what is worthy of striving for.

Whether it is a teacher, a close friend, a mentor at work, or a public figure whose character you respect, these individuals often serve as blueprints for your own behavior. From them, you learn not only specific skills or knowledge but also the underlying values and philosophies that guide their actions. For example, a teacher who goes above and beyond to support struggling students so they too may experience success may ignite in you a passion for helping others. A colleague who rises above others in demonstrating leadership in exceptional guiding, coaching, and teamwork can teach you how to collaborate and inspire others. Positive role models help you shape your own goals, approaches, and mindset.

While learning from those who excel is invaluable, equally significant are the lessons you gain from observing the missteps of others. In fact, some of the most powerful lessons in life come from the mistakes you make or witness in others. These experiences teach you what to avoid, helping you to navigate potential pitfalls before you encounter them yourselves. For instance, observing someone who reacts impulsively and suffers the consequences may prompt you to reflect on the importance of patience and thoughtful decision-making. Watching a leader who lacks the ability to understand and resonate with the needs and perspectives of others faces a loss of trust within their team can help you appreciate the critical role of empathy in leadership.

This form of learning is compelling. It reminds you that you do not have to make every mistake yourselves in order to understand its consequences. By paying attention to the choices others make, whether right or wrong, you gain the foresight to avoid certain traps. In essence, the failures and flaws of others are not wasted moments; they are opportunities for both them and you to sharpen your judgment and build a more resilient, thoughtful approach to life.

First impressions matter, but they should not define everything.

My mother—your great-grandmother, Charles and Isabelle—was a great storyteller. My favorite stories are ones about her early life living on a farm with her family. However, she often shared this one from our own early childhood: After spending fifty-two years in Brazil, my mother's great-uncle, Karam, returned to Lebanon in 1965 when I was four, my older brother, Wadih was six, and the two younger brothers Bassam and Sami, were three and one, respectively. Our youngest brother, Roland, had not yet been born. Once he had a chance to meet and briefly observe us, Jeddo (Grandpa) Karam, as we called him, quickly gave us all nicknames based on our personalities as he saw them. I was the *calm*. Wadih, the *impolite*. Bassam, the *fiery*. And Sami, the *Warwar*, a colorful bee-eater bird common in Lebanon. To the day she died, if asked to describe her children, my mother in agreement with its sentiments, would retell this story.

First impressions are often seen as the most vivid defining moments in human interaction. Whether it is a first date, a job interview, or meeting a stranger, people tend to form opinions quickly. The idea that a first impression is a lasting impression reflects the notion that the initial perception someone forms about you often endures beyond the moment itself. Studies suggest that people often make judgments about others within the first few seconds of meeting them, based on factors like appearance, body language, and tone of voice. These early judgments influence how you may interact with someone over time. In professional settings, for instance, an employer may base their decision largely on how a candidate presents themselves initially, sometimes outweighing the candidate's actual skills or long-term potential. First impressions are resistant to change because information you learn first is weighted more heavily than information you learn later. This means that even if someone changes their behavior over time, you may still cling to your original perception of them.

While a first impression holds true in many cases, it is also important to recognize the limitations and exceptions to it. There are several powerful defining moments in human interaction—moments that shape relationships, trust, and understanding between people—that offer more accurate impressions. For instance, when someone lends you sincere support during a difficult time or offers a listening ear, takes time to help you with a difficult school project, stays late at work to help you or someone else with a task, or you simply observe a person giving up their seat on public transportation. Such acts of kindness can better define how you see others, perhaps even overriding a weak or awkward first impression you had of them. Similarly, a heartfelt apology after a mistake can be a defining moment that builds trust and demonstrates personal integrity. These small, but meaningful actions, can make a lasting and meaningful difference, better define how you view someone, and offer a clearer view into their values.

On the other hand, negative actions like disrespect or betrayal can also become defining moments, even if someone initially gave a good impression. A person who breaks your trust or acts selfishly may quickly change how you view them, proving that first impressions are not always lasting. Furthermore, how someone handles conflict, whether with calmness and respect, or with hostility and anger, can also reveal how you perceive their true nature. These experiences illustrate that while first impressions matter, they are only one of many defining moments that shape human relationships. People are complex and constantly evolving, and it is essential to remain open-minded and allow relationships to develop organically. One moment, especially the first, should never define a person entirely.

Also, cultural differences are always a factor. In a diverse world where people come from different cultures, backgrounds, and communication styles, it is easy to misinterpret someone's behavior. What might seem rude or disinterested in one culture could be a sign of respect or shyness in another. That is why relying too heavily on first impressions can lead to unfair biases or stereotypes. As someone who came to America from a different country, with a different culture and language, I have experienced this firsthand. Even though I learned and perfected English subsequent to my arrival here, and those who know me well and know my story often comment positively on my oral and written communication skills, and cite my faint and all but disappearing accent. In fact, it is not unusual for my native-born colleagues to volunteer me for assignments that require strong speaking and writing abilities. Yet, in other settings, I have been told at times by others "I did not understand a single word you said" immediately after saying something, perhaps as a way to dismiss a position I hold or an argument I made.

As you spend more time with others, you develop a richer understanding of their character, behavior, and values, which can either reinforce or completely change your initial views. People have layers and evolve constantly; a single interaction rarely captures who they really are. Remain open-minded and allow time for deeper understanding.

The kitchen is more than it seems.

Moving to the United States taught me to develop both practical and personal skills, ranging from the consequential to the essential and from the important to the mundane. Growing up in Lebanon, my brothers and I rarely recognized how much our parents would go out of their way to do all they could for us. They prioritized our time and energy for what they believed mattered more, schoolwork, for example. That changed quickly when I got here. Cooking was one of the essentials I needed to take up first, out of sheer necessity.

To my surprise, I enjoyed it, and I became good at it. Having five boys must have had at least one drawback as far as my mother was concerned: lack of help in the kitchen. While I was not much of a cook then, I did spend time on Sundays and holidays in the kitchen keeping my mother's company and helping her with some minor preparation as she labored to make traditional family meals for us and other family and friends who usually joined us. What I learned from those moments, even from the minor tasks, gave me the confidence to start handling things myself when the time came, promptly after my arrival in the United States.

Its utility lasted beyond my expectation. As our family was growing, cooking was a way for me to assist your grandmother, Maura, with household chores. But it also became a meaningful outlet for me to relieve stress, and it often turned into a shared family activity. From an early age, my daughter, your Aunt Rebecca, and I spent a great deal of time together in the kitchen. We frequently found ourselves at odds over recipes. I enjoyed experimenting with ingredients and adjusting measurements, while she preferred to adhere strictly to the written instructions. To make her case, she would emphasize the care and precision that went into developing and testing those recipes. I, on the other hand, believed that once a recipe was in our hands, it became our own—something we could adapt and personalize to suit our tastes, asserting to Rebecca that it was our recipe and we could make it what we want. Eventually, we managed to reach a compromise. We developed a mutually agreeable approach: I would be able to make reasonable modifications without excessive creativity, while she became receptive to making adjustments to the recipe without strictly following every detail.

While life is usually described as a journey, perhaps a more accurate comparison might be to a recipe—a unique blend of preparation, ingredients, seasoning, and efforts that you, as the *chef de cuisine*, have the power of control and creation. No one else can dictate how you should live your lives, because it is your recipe, and you have the freedom to make it your own. From the choices you make every day to the larger decisions that define your paths, the ingredients are yours to select. These ingredients represent the different elements that make up your experiences—your values, passions, relationships, and aspirations. The beauty of this perspective is that it makes you the designer of your own experiences. It acts as a reminder that your life is not a formula, but a dynamic dish that you can adjust, season, and entirely reimagine to reflect the person you truly are, or who you seek to become.

My point is that you have the power to choose what goes into the recipe of your lives, and there is no universally correct blend. What matters is that you are choosing ingredients that embody your principles, what you like, and what you want to create. For example, your careers might reflect a desire for social impact or financial stability, or perhaps a balance of both. If you value creativity, you might choose to include time pursuing artistic endeavors. If family and connection are important to you, you can prioritize spending time with loved ones and invest in relationships with those who you enjoy and appreciate.

Creating your lives' recipe is not about combining all your ingredients together in a random way. It requires understanding proportions and the way various parts relate and respond to one another. Too much of a certain ingredient can overpower the rest and lead to an imbalanced result. For example, focusing solely on your career advancement while neglecting your health or relationships may leave your lives feeling incomplete, even if you achieve professional success. On the other hand, if you devote all your time to pursuing personal interests or socializing without appropriate attention to your career, financial security, or intellectual development can also result in a sense of unfulfillment.

Equally important is that your lives' recipe can shift and adapt as needed. You can adjust and experiment with different combinations to create the result you desire. You might find that certain ingredients such as work, family, or leisure need to be included in different proportions at different points in your lives. As you grow and evolve, your recipe may need to change too. That is not just expected, but fundamental.

Empathy teaches us to value others.

Empathy is the ability to understand and care about how others feel, even if their experience is different from ours. It involves putting ourselves in the shoes of others to see how their circumstances, decisions, and behaviors have shaped them. By doing so, we gain a better understanding of human nature and more insight into the complexity of the world we navigate.

For this to happen, you need to step outside your own perspective and imagine the emotions, thoughts, and experiences of others, especially when they might be different from your own. It is not a trivial process, but with intention, empathy can be nurtured.

The beauty of this form of learning—to decipher the "what" and the "why" about the feelings of others—is that it teaches you many lessons that are often beautifully interwoven. First, seeing the world through someone else's eyes helps you to be kind and caring. Second, noticing when someone may be in distress and offering them support without being asked helps you develop intuition. Third, listening closely when someone is going through a hard time, even if you do not have the same problem, helps you become attentive. And, finally, thinking carefully about how you might choose to act when someone is in a difficult situation, even when it is not the easiest thing to do, teaches you to be generous. Speaking up when you see someone being treated unfairly and helping them feel heard is a pinnacle act of kindness and a most profound lesson you can learn.

Empathy helps you be better friends, siblings, and people. It helps make the world a kinder place, and it makes you feel good inside, too. It is a powerful way to build connections, resolve conflicts, and support others. Like any skill, the more you practice it, the better you get at it.

I am so proud of you both, no matter your age, and I know you will continue to grow into kind, thoughtful individuals. Also, remember the dedication of this book: I count on you to lead the way for the next generation of Deeks and to help those who come after you, your siblings and cousins, or others who may need your help, when they are here.

As I bring this letter to a close, Charles and Isabelle, I do so with a deep sense of appreciation for a long and meaningful journey. I began with little more than hope in my pocket and the values instilled by my parents, whose love was fierce and sacrificial. They gave without measure so their children might dream without limits. I carried their legacy in every decision I have made, in every door I walked through, and in every moment I chose to rise when it would have been easier to rest.

Before I close, Charles and Isabelle, I would like to share with you a beautiful memory from my childhood. Let me call it the red-flag-on-the-balcony. This flag was both a literal and symbolic beacon that my mother, your great-grandmother, invented out of practicality to draw my brothers and me back home for a meal or to shield us from the midday summer heat at the beach. This simple system of communication, long before phones and texts, became an emotional marker of homecoming tied to unity and belonging. This quiet childhood signal still echoes instinctively as my mental image of a flag bidding me to return home.

When you are older and have children of your own, you might consider hanging the red flag, a sign that someone is home.

Everyone, Charles and Isabelle, is precious.

With all my love,

Jeddo

ABOUT THE AUTHOR

FADI P. DEEK, PhD, is Distinguished Professor of Informatics and Mathematical Sciences at New Jersey Institute of Technology. He received his BS and MS in Computer Science, and PhD in Computer and Information Science—all from NJIT. Dr. Deek has also served NJIT in a wide range of leadership roles, culminating in a decade as Provost and Senior Executive Vice President. Prior to this, he served as Dean for the College of Science and Liberal Arts, also for a decade. Dr. Deek is the author/co-author of six books, fourteen book chapters, and more than 200 scholarly publications in journals and conference proceedings. He is also the editor/co-editor of five edited collections. In addition to his commitment to science and technology education and research, Dr. Deek is an activist for peace and prosperity in Lebanon and for all of its citizens.